Communicating

With Your

CAT

Full-color photos, illustrations, and a glossary

J. Anne Helgren

BARRON'S

Acknowledgments

I would like to thank Grace Freedson, Mary Falcon, and Lynne Vessie (Barron's Educational Series, Inc.) for all their invaluable help and guidance; Amy Shojai and the Cat Writers' Association; Michael Kaufman and Karen Rosa of the American Humane Association for their help with the Cats on Stage chapter; Tyler Stratton of SmartPractice; and Michael Mullen at StarKist Foods for permission to reprint the cat aging chart. I also thank Darlene Arden, Elisabeth Basore, Rose Basore, Arlene Evans, Bill Helgren, Jude Lowell, Betty Roby, and Susan Scheibel for their help, support, and advice. Last but certainly not least, I thank BigCat, Bitty, Punkin, Pooka, Goose, Clancy, Spook, and all the other cats that have helped me understand the unique feline nature.

All inquiries should be addressed to:
Barron's Educational Series, Inc.
250 Wireless Boulevard
Hauppauge, New York 11788
http://www.barronseduc.com

Library of Congress Catalog Card No. 99-27043

International Standard Book No. 0-7641-0855-7

Library of Congress Cataloging-in-Publication Data
Helgren, J. Anne.
    Communicating with your cat / J. Anne Helgren.
        p. cm.
    Includes bibliographical references.
    ISBN 0-7641-0855-7 (pbk. : alk. paper)
    1. Cats—Training.   2. Cats—Behavior.
3. Human-animal communication. I. Title.
    SF446.5.H45   1999
    636.8'088'7—dc21
                                                        99-27043
                                                        CIP

Printed in Hong Kong

9 8 7 6 5 4 3 2 1

Cover Photos
Norvia Behling

Photo Credits

Norvia Behling: pages x, 11, 13, 16, 17, 19, 22, 25, 26, 30, 33–38, 42, 45, 52, 56, 57, 59, 61–63, 67, 68, 71, 75, 78, 80, 83, 85, 89, 93, 97, 98, 100, 101, 103, 104, 109, 110, 116, 120, 121, 124–130, 132–136, 152, 155, 157; J. Anne Helgren: pages 23, 49, 137; Bob Schwartz: pages 1, 4–6, 8; SmartPractice: pages 105, 118 (Tyler Stratton).

Illustration Credits

Michele Earle-Bridges: pages 2, 7, 12, 14, 15, 22, 24, 27, 39, 64, 76, 77, 90, 96, 102, 115; Tana Hakanson-Monsalve: page 60; David Wenzel: page 23.

About the Author

J. Anne Helgren has written five books on cats for Barron's Educational Series, and is a contributor to *CATS* magazine. She has written the featured breed profiles for *CATS* magazine since 1992, for which she was awarded Certificates of Excellence from the Cat Writers' Association in 1994 and 1996, and for which she won the Muse Medallion award in 1997. She is a professional member of the Cat Writers' Association and the Dog Writers' Association, and has written dozens of articles on cats and other companion animals for national and regional magazines and newspapers. She also serves as an editorial consultant for Barron's Educational Series, for whom she edits and critiques cat-related manuscripts and proposals. Ms. Helgren lives near Sacramento, California, with her husband, Bill, and five feline friends.

Important Note

When you handle cats, you may sometimes get scratched or bitten. If this happens, have a doctor treat the injuries immediately.

Make sure your cat receives all the necessary shots and dewormings, otherwise serious danger to the animal and to human health may arise. A few diseases and parasites can be communicated to humans. If your cat shows any signs of illness, you should definitely consult a veterinarian. If you are worried about your own health, see your doctor and tell him or her that you have cats.

Some people have allergic reactions to cats. If you think you might be allergic, see your doctor before you get a cat.

It is possible for a cat to cause damage to someone else's property and even to cause accidents. For your own protection you should make sure your insurance covers such eventualities, and you should definitely have liability insurance.

Contents

Preface

I remember the day I learned to communicate with cats. I was in bed, sick with a migraine, and as usual, Bitty, my Siamese in a tabby suit, was playing nurse, curled up beside my pillow comforting me with her purr as she had done so many times before. But something different happened that night. Bitty stood up and, giving me her attention-commanding Siamese yowl, looked at me with an expression I'd never seen before. Her eyes were full of intelligence and insight far beyond what I'd thought possible. Suddenly, I was not looking into the eyes of a cat but into the soul of a fellow being, and for just a moment the barriers between our two species fell away. She seemed to look right into my soul; for a moment we were equals, she and I, sharing an understanding and empathy so deep that language was unnecessary.

At any rate, the moment passed, and Bitty settled down again to purr on my pillow, but that day our relationship changed subtly. We developed a closer bond and depended upon each other in a way we hadn't before. Now, wherever I am, Bitty is too; she's developed an uncanny ability to read my emotions and respond to them, and I to hers. Perhaps we always had this ability but never had the insight necessary to put it in practice. That special bond is still just as strong today. Until Bitty, I didn't realize true communication between two very different species was possible.

Cats need to be needed, just as humans need to do useful and fulfilling work. We are really more alike than we think. Stephen J. O'Brien, a contributor to the Human Genome Project, notes that virtually every cat gene has a human counterpart, and the sequence of the DNA in the two species is so similar that it's possible to determine which gene is which just by comparing their DNA sequences. Perhaps this is the reason that humankind has been fascinated by cats for thousands of years. At current count, cats outnumber dogs in the United States 66 million to 55 million. Their clean and quiet ways make them the ideal pet for the busy, mobile pet owner. However, they are still largely misunderstood.

My special relationship with Bitty also confirmed my suspicion that cats are a lot smarter than they let on, and moved me to explore the mysteries of the cat's mind a bit more closely. What I learned surprised, delighted, and amazed

A Note About Pronouns

Many cat lovers (including this one) feel that the neuter pronoun "it" is not appropriate when applied to our feline friends; therefore, in this book, you'll notice that the chapters alternate between a female cat named Fluffy and a male cat named Tiger. This is to avoid the clumsy use of "he or she" when referring to cats, since the English language doesn't have a gender-neutral pronoun that can be used to refer to cats—and to people. This technique is designed to show that no sexism is intended, and to support Barron's goal of avoiding sexist language in our books.

me. In this book we'll explore the mysteries of the feline mind and body, and you'll learn how you can develop a human/feline bond for your, and your cat's, benefit and enjoyment. You'll learn how cats think, why they behave the way they do, and how you can understand and interpret your cat's language to improve your cat-owning experience. You'll also learn that cats can indeed be trained and will gain skills that will help you shape your cat's behavior.

Dedicated to Libby Basore, who taught me to love animals, and to Bitty, who taught me that communication was possible.

—J. Anne Helgren

Introduction

Intelligence Versus Instinct

Do cats think? Any cat lover asked this question would instantly respond, "Well, of course they do!" People who have had the pleasure of sharing their lives with felines know that cats are capable of intelligent reasoning. Even when you take into account that cat lovers often attribute human characteristics to their cats, the evidence does point in that direction. Cats have powers of reasoning and use them for their benefit; a cat that comes running at the sound of the refrigerator being opened is not behaving on instinct. She has learned that food is in there, and she has applied the knowledge to her advantage. She has learned and remembered. That takes thought and reasoning.

In the past, humankind—or certain members of the species, anyway—puffed up with imagined superiority, declared that humans think, and that that quality separates humans from animals. René Descartes (1596–1650), dissatisfied with the arbitrary methods of science used in his day, was determined to discover a method of reasoning applicable to all natural sciences. Finding that the sciences rested on disputed philosophical ideas, he set out to discover a first principle, which could not be doubted, on which to build the knowledge of humankind. That first principle was the immortalized "I think, therefore I am."

This was fine, as far as it went; however, Descartes thought that it only applied to humankind. He, like many other theologians and philosophers, believed that, unlike humans, animals were nothing more than automatons, unthinking machines that reacted to their environments by mere instinct, unable to reason and without free will. In fact, the word "behavior" was rarely applied to the actions of animals before 1900. They were said to display "instincts, habits, manners, and customs," not behavior, which would imply consciousness.

Charles Darwin (1809–1882), on the other hand, credited with developing the theory of evolution, thought "the difference in mind between man and the higher animals, great as it is, certainly is one of degree and not of kind." He believed that animals possessed powers of reasoning.

Cats are clever and adaptable, and capable of intelligent reasoning.

In the debate over intelligence versus instinct, the problem is not merely that researchers thought cats—or any animals—used instinct to guide their behavior. That isn't in dispute. It was the black or white thinking that an animal must operate on one system or the other—it must have intelligence, or it must have instinct, but not both—that caused animals to be considered unthinking. Intelligence is also a matter of human perception. As American writer Will Cuppy said, "If a cat does something, we call it instinct; if we do the same thing, for the same reason, we call it intelligence."

Cats, like humans, like all animals, use both their instinct and their intelligence. Biology shapes behavior, instinct drives basic needs, and environment and early learning shape the final product. It's a combination of nature and nurture, just as it is with humans. We are not really all that different from the species with which we share this planet. It is, as Darwin said, a matter of degree.

Cats and Dogs

Poet T. S. Eliot, in his *Old Possum's Book of Practical Cats,* gives us this bit of feline wisdom:

> Again I must remind you that
> A Dog's a Dog—A CAT'S A CAT.

When communicating with your cat, the first thing you must learn is that cats behave exactly like cats and not at all like dogs; therefore, expecting them to behave like dogs will get you into trouble with your feline friends.

You might hear any number of discussions about the relative intelligence of cats and dogs, as though some sort of contest were being waged, the winner to be deemed the Top Companion Animal. It's pretty silly, because both dogs and cats make great pets, but in completely different ways. This is not surprising, since they are completely different animals.

Dogs make wonderful, loyal, and valuable companions. They perform many useful services: They pull sleds over snowy expanses, herd livestock, serve as the eyes of the blind and the ears of the deaf, help wage the war on drugs with their keen noses—the list goes on and on.

So why, folks ask, can't cats learn to do all those things? Cats must, these folks reason, be less intelligent than dogs. Such "intelligence tests" are unfair. It is like saying that because horses cannot fly like birds, they must be less intelligent than birds. If the test of intelligence were to right oneself in midair, run along the top of a fence without falling, or rid a barn of rodents, the cat would win. And cat owners happily point out that refusing to cooperate with any silly intelligence tests is surely a sign of the cat's high intelligence.

The problem with intelligence tests is that they are thought up by humans and are used to test abilities that humans find useful or important—and that intelligence tests themselves are of dubious value. Experts can't agree on their value and fairness to *humans,* let alone to animals. Nature's intelligence test is the only one that really matters—is the animal smart enough to survive?

At any rate, cats do not behave like dogs for the same reason that horses do not fly, fish gallop, or turtles sprint—they are different species with different genetic programming and motivational imperatives. This may seem pretty obvious, but it's amazing how many people seem to forget this point when trying to get their cats to perform certain behaviors.

Cats and dogs diverged as separate species some 50 million years ago and are now different in many fundamental ways. In addition, dogs have been domesticated for much longer than have cats. A 50,000-year-old cave painting in Europe shows a doglike animal hunting with humans, indicating that dogs probably have been sharing their lives with humans for many thousands of years. Cats, on the other hand, have been domesticated about 5,000 years, give or take, and are never truly owned in the same way that a dog belongs to her master or mistress. Dogs also have been bred for hundreds of years for particular traits that humans find useful. Cats have not. Their useful trait (to humans) is to rid dwellings of rodents, a behavior that comes naturally to them. They need no training from us to do it; in fact, if training is not your thing, cats need little training to make good household companions. All you need to do is point out the litter box and the scratching post, and Fluffy usually does the rest. Usually.

The wild ancestors of dogs were pack hunters. Wolves and other wild relatives of the dog hunt in packs, and dogs have retained the instincts associated with pack behavior. Loyalty to and cooperation with the pack is very important to the pack's survival and, therefore, dogs learn early in life to put the pack before personal wants and needs. The pack leader plays a vital role in the pack's survival, and this individual doles out discipline as needed, maintains order among the members, organizes the hunts, controls the breeding in the pack, and so on. Receiving discipline from a dominant packmate is an accepted part of pack behavior, and is learned early in life.

Accepting Discipline

Cats are not pack animals. They have no emotional imperative that drives them to *obey* dominant members of their species—stay out of the way of, or run away from, yes, but not *obey*. Accepting discipline from another member of her species—other than her mother—is alien to a cat. A cat receiving a swipe from another cat learns to stay away from that individual in the future, not to jump through hoops for it. That's why negative reinforcement doesn't work on cats.

Also, cats are solitary hunters; they are not genetically programmed to cooperate with the group in obtaining food. Except for the mother's protection of her young, cats make their own decisions, learn from their own mistakes, and perform behaviors that benefit them personally. This does not make them more selfish than dogs, although that trait is often attributed to them. These are the survival lessons nature has taught them, and they've learned them well. Dogs will fight to defend their packs, or the people whom they have accepted as their packs. To a dog, defending the pack means survival. A cat will fight to defend her own life; a cat neither receives nor expects help from other members of her species. There's an exception to this, of course: A mother cat will fight most viciously for the lives of her kittens, and that's survival instinct, too.

With this in mind, therefore, it's really not surprising that cats do not respond to the kind of conditioning effective with dogs. Dogs respond well to consistent praise and authoritative correction, but authoritative correction has no place in cat training. You will never teach a cat to do anything she doesn't really want to do. As a tiger trainer once commented, "You can't *make* a tiger do anything."

Despite their solitary hunting habits and independence, cats are social animals and are capable of close, loving relationships with their human and feline friends. The key to cat training is to develop a trusting relationship with Fluffy, and then convince her that certain behaviors produce pleasurable results while other behaviors produce unpleasant ones.

So how intelligent are cats? Very smart—about being cats.

Chapter One
Your Cat's Origins

And let me touch those curving claws of yellow ivory, and grasp the tail that like a monstrous asp coils round your heavy velvet paws.
—Oscar Wilde

In sheer numbers, cats outnumber dogs as pets in the United States today. It's their strength of personality and self-confidence, along with their grace, beauty, clean ways, and affectionate natures, that make them a popular choice for many animal lovers. They are also one of the least understood companion animals, and this can cause any number of problems between owner and cat. A good understanding of the way cats think, and why they think that way, will help you have a more positive relationship with your feline friend.

Just because cats have deigned to share their lives with humans doesn't mean they have lost those 35 million years of evolutionary adaptation. Cats are among the most successful predators the world has ever known, and that kitty purring happily in your lap is no exception. Most cat species share similar traits, and the domestic cat's wild origins affect its behavior today. In many ways, it's still a wild cat in domestic cat clothing.

Felines act in ways that can seem strange to us, but that's because we don't understand the way cats think and communicate. Understanding where your cat has been, in an evolutionary sense, gives you a better understanding of where your cat is today, and why Tiger behaves as he does.

Saber-toothed cats evolved around 35 million years ago. Extinct now, some saber-toothed cats such as Smilodon californicus *were still alive as recently as 13,000 years ago.*

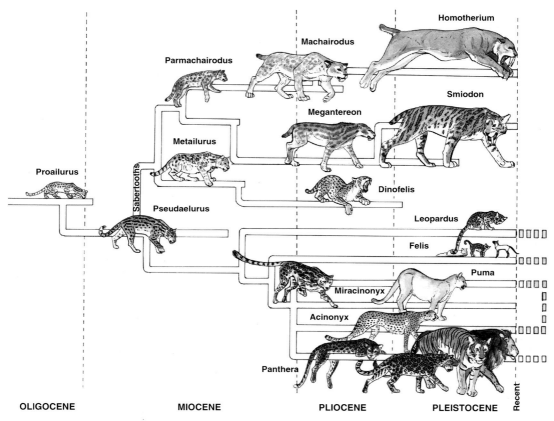

Through modern DNA testing and analysis, scientists have substantially changed their theories about how the cat family developed. The first true cat is now thought to be Proailurus.

Evolution

Although the cat's journey to its present form began around 35 million years ago, the earliest known true cat is called *Proailurus,* a 20-some-pound (approximately 9 kg) predator that lived during the Oligocene, around 25 million years ago. It's thought that *Proailurus* hunted small mammals but spent about half its time up in trees, a refuge from the larger ground-dwelling predators. Eventually, *Proailurus* became extinct, but before it did, a species called *Pseudaelurus* split from its evolutionary line. *Pseudaelurus* lived in the early Miocene, about 20 million years ago. After myriad millennia, *Pseudaelurus,* too, became extinct, but not before two separate branches grew from this family tree. One branch developed into cats with bigger teeth, including the saber-toothed cats. None of the cats from this branch exists today, although some saber-toothed cats such as *Smilodon fatalis* were still around as recently as 10,000 years ago, roaming the hills and valleys of Hollywood, California, and the rest of the Los Angeles basin. That's not to imply that saber-tooths were not effective predators; the last 10,000 years is almost the only time in the last 11 million years that a saber-toothed cat hasn't prowled the earth.

Two theories exist about the extinction of these cats. One theory suggests that climate and vegetation changes caused the extinction of the saber-tooths' prey, which, in turn, caused the cats' extinction. This is an example of the danger of over-specialization; if an animal relies too heavily on a particular prey or certain environmental conditions, changes can make a species obsolete. The other theory agrees with the "extinction of prey" theory, but places the extinction of the prey upon which the felines depended at humankind's door.

The other branch of the cat family tree, however, was more successful at adapting, and from this branch came our 38 modern-day cat species. In the late Miocene (about 10 million years ago), the modern-day cats began to evolve. It was, in fact, a great age for all of the mammals. Forests changed into broad plains of edible foliage, and the large herds of herbivores allowed cats to refine their hunting skills. In this feline branch, the canine teeth became smaller, but the cats became smarter and faster, one of the reasons, but not the only one, for their survival. Adaptability has always been one of the cat's handiest abilities, and has allowed them to survive environmental changes.

One remarkable thing about the cat's evolution is that *Proailurus,* the cat family's first true ancestor, was in many basic ways very much like our modern-day cat species. In 25 million years of evolution, other animals—including the human one—have evolved to the point where their ancestors look little or nothing like the modern version. That's because the evolutionary changes were necessary for survival as the climates, wildlife, and vegetation around them transformed. With cats, however, the basic structure has not changed in 25 million years. Why? Because the basic design—the fang and claw, the agility, flexible backbone, and muscular strength—was an effective design. Cats, even 25 million years ago, were well-designed and efficient hunters, and as a family they were able to survive the changes each epoch brought. That's the reason a study of the cat's ancestors and modern-day relatives teaches us so much about the behavior of our domestic cats—under the skin, they are all very similar, and domestic cats have not lost touch with their wild origins.

The Cat Family

Taxonomists, scientists who classify living organisms, have substantially revised the classification of the cat family, *Felidae,* due to the recent analysis of feline DNA. In this genetic analysis, researchers compared blood samples from our present-day felids to discover relationships between groups of cats. Through this research, 10 distinct evolutionary families have been identified to classify our 38 cat species. These groups split from one another about 10 to 15 million years ago. Domestic cats and their nearest relatives have been around for about two million years, relative newcomers in the evolution of the felids.

The table on page 5 shows the current thinking about the cat classifications. For each species, both the common name, for example, domestic cat, and the scientific name, for example, *Felis catus,* are given.

Differences in Cat Species

The cat species have obvious differences in size, markings, habitat, hunting habits, choice of prey, social structures, and so on. For example, the Pantherines or great cats are known for the differences in construction of the vocal apparatus. The hyoid bone at the base of the tongue is partially made of cartilage in the great cats, which gives the vocal apparatus the mobility necessary to produce roaring sounds.

Less obviously, all cats, including our domestic buddies, have many similarities—more similarities than differences, in fact. The smallest house cat and the largest lion have much in common; think of your pet as a tiny tiger. For one thing, all of the cat species have meager or no collarbones, which gives the front legs a great deal of flexibility. The spine is loosely connected and very flexible, and the body is long and has great muscular strength, allowing for agility and great bursts of speed. The characteristic cat slink is created by this arrangement. The face is broad and the jaw short, which allows for a more powerful bite in the cat than in an animal with long jaws. The cat has fewer teeth than any other carnivore, but all

Panthera leo, *the lion. The lion is of the panther lineage that includes the tiger, jaguar, leopard, snow leopard, and clouded leopard. These cats are called "Pantherines."*

Cat Classifications

Domestic Cat Lineage
Domestic cat *Felis catus*
Pallas's cat *Otocolobus manul*
Chinese desert cat *Felis bieti*
Sand cat *Felis margarita*
Black-footed cat *Felis nigripes*
Jungle cat *Felis chaus*
Wildcat *Felis silvestris*

Ocelot Lineage
Ocelot *Leopardus pardalis*
Margay *Leopardus wiedii*
Kodkod *Oncifelis guigna*
Mountain cat *Oreailurus jacobita*
Geoffrey's cat *Oncifelis geoffreyi*
Pampas cat *Oncifelis colocolo*
Oncilla (the tiger cat) *Leopardus tigrinus*

Caracal Lineage
Caracal *Caracal caracal*
African golden cat *Profelis aurata*

Asian Leopard Cat Lineage
Fishing cat *Prionailurus viverrinus*
Iriomote cat *Mayailurus iriomotensis*
Leopard cat *Prionailurus bengalensis*
Flat-headed cat *Prionailurus planiceps*

Panther Lineage
Lion *Panthera leo*
Tiger *Panthera tigris*
Jaguar *Panthera onca*
Snow leopard *Uncia uncia*
Leopard *Panthera pardus*
Clouded leopard *Neofelis nebulosa*

Puma Lineage
Puma (also called the mountain lion and cougar) *Puma concolor*
Cheetah *Acinonyx jubatus*
Jaguarundi *Herpailurus yaguarondi*

Serval Lineage
Serval *Leptailurus serval*

Rusty-spotted Cat Lineage
Rusty-spotted cat *Prionailurus rubiginosus*

Bay Cat Lineage
Bay cat *Catopuma badia*
Temminck's golden cat *Catopuma temmincki*

Lynx Lineage
Bobcat *Lynx rufus*
Canada lynx *Lynx canadensis*
Marbled cat *Pardofelis marmorata*
Eurasian lynx *Lynx lynx*
Iberian lynx *Lynx pardinus*

Felis silvestris libyca, **the ancestor of all domestic cats.**

Acinonyx jubatus, *the cheetah. Current DNA studies show that cheetahs are closely related to mountain lions, also called cougars or pumas.*

the cat's teeth are designed to cut and shear meat, making its bite very deadly. Rough sandpaperlike tongues rasp meat off bones. All cats except the cheetah have a truly marvelous digital arrangement—needlesharp retractable claws are safely sheathed when not in use, cutting down on wear and tear, but ready to whip out instantly when needed. Their eyes are large and close together to give them acute binocular vision; keen night vision helps them find and catch their nocturnal prey.

Out of the 38 species of cats, great and small, 37 have declined or are currently in decline due to hunting, disappearing habitat, and reduction of prey. Some probably will, in fact, become extinct in the future. The only cat species in no immediate danger of extinction is *Felis catus,* the domestic cat.

The Domestic Cat's Origins

The domestic cat most likely arose from the species *Felis silvestris,* in particular the subspecies African wildcat *Felis silvestris libyca* (also spelled *lybica*). Put side to side, you might have a difficult time distinguishing the African wildcat from your domestic house cat. The African wildcat does have differences, but they are hard to spot unless you are an expert in such things. The African wildcat is slightly larger, but that simply means to the layperson that it looks like a slightly larger domestic cat. Native to Africa, Western Asia, Scotland, and Southern Europe, the African wildcat has the same structure and number of chromosomes as the domestic cat. *Felis silvestris libyca* interbreeds easily with domestic cats, so easily, in fact, that it's on the brink of extinction as a pure species. Unlike other wildcats, *Felis silvestris libyca* is comparatively easy to domesticate and often chooses to live near human communities. Many of the mummified cat remains from the cat cult that existed some 4,000 years ago in Egypt are *Felis silvestris libyca*. Since Egypt is considered the first place that cats were kept as companions rather than as the perfect mousetrap, evidence does point to this species as the origin of *Felis catus*.

Domestication

Cats were one of the last animals to be domesticated, one reason they retain many of their natural behaviors and instincts. Cats have been "tamed" for only a few thousand years and have always accepted our domination with reservations. The cat has kept its self-confidence and strong, spirited personality, and that's one reason that humans respond to them so strongly—in both positive and negative ways.

Humans learned that felines were invaluable in controlling the rodent populations that destroyed their food supplies, and cats discovered how handy humans were in attracting tasty rodents.

Before humans settled down to an agricultural existence, and while they still lived as "hunter-gatherers," they domesticated animals such as goats, pigs, and sheep so they could transport with them a ready supply of food. Dogs became allies in hunting and in defending the animal herds from predators. Estimates vary, but it is thought dogs were domesticated around 20,000 years ago, although some research suggests that the relationship between dogs and humans began some 100,000 years ago. Being animals that form packs to cooperate in hunting efforts, dogs were more easily domesticated than cats. Cats,

The Egyptian cat cult existed for almost 2,000 years, finally ending in 390 A.D. by Imperial decree. Thousands of cat figurines, amulets, mummies, statues, and paintings still exist, testaments to the cat's popularity and significance in early Egyptian culture.

being solitary hunters, were less easily tamed.

Around 10,000 years ago, when humans moved from being hunter-gatherers to being members of settled communities, cats may have learned that humans provided a reliable food source—the vermin attracted to the food supplies. In effect, these cats exploited a newly formed ecological niche, as did the mice and rats that learned that humans provided large tasty stores of food around their settlements. For a time, estimated to be between 9,000 and 4,000 years ago, cats lived in a semidomestic state, eating the vermin around and in human settlements without truly becoming domestic animals.

We don't yet clearly understand the process of domestication. It appears to have a genetic basis and can be inherited, because the docile behavior and dependency of domestic animals develop after years of selective breeding. A recent study supports this theory; the offspring of friendly and unfriendly male cats were studied, and it was found that the offspring of the friendly cats inherited their fathers' amicable natures. Close association with their fathers was not a factor in shaping this behavior, since the kittens had no contact with their male parents.

It is likely that, from selective breeding, cats developed into the domesticated animals they are today. The cats that hung around humans interbred and passed along their human-friendly genes. Those individuals that were less adaptable to life with humans left for less inhabited regions, and only the human-friendly cats stayed to mate and pass along their domestic dispositions.

After the process of domestication began, humans began to see cats as much more than slinking nocturnal animals wary of humankind. Humans learned that felines were invaluable in controlling the rodent populations that destroyed their crops and food supplies around the same time that cats discovered how handy humans were in attracting tasty rodents.

The Spread of the Feline

Since *Felis libyca* came from Africa and Southern Europe, it's logical to assume that feline domestication first occurred in those areas. The Egyptians were the first people to leave records of their alliance with cats. Cats became household companions to the Egyptians about 4,000 years ago, as evidenced by Egyptian writings and the depictions of cats on ornaments, statues, bas-reliefs, and paintings. Although presumably cats were first welcomed for their rodent-catching abilities, later they were treated as beloved household companions, and then as the physical manifestations of gods.

The Egyptians were fiercely protective of their cats, but eventually, Phoenician traders transported felines to Europe and the British Isles, where the cats were used to control rodent populations. Romans smuggled cats out of Egypt and brought them along into conquered regions such as France, Germany, Holland, England, and Spain. Monks transported cats to the Orient. Slowly, domestic cats spread. By the birth of Christ, many cultures, such as those of the Japanese, Siamese, East Indians, and Chinese, had come to appreciate felines for their beauty, wisdom, and usefulness.

But not all cultures appreciated cats. Beginning around the middle of the thirteenth century, religious sects in Europe persecuted and killed cats for a supposed link with the devil. Mass purges required that cats be rounded up and destroyed, and ritualistic ceremonies were held to symbolize casting out evil by the killing of cats. In the 1300s, when cats would have been tremendously useful in reducing the rodent populations that spread the bubonic plague, the persecution was at its worst. Rodents and their fleas flourished at this time and with them so did the Black Death, which from 1347 to 1351 A.D. killed one third to one half the population of Europe.

With the advent of sailing ships, domestic cats spread. It was thought that having cats aboard ship brought good luck; therefore, cats spread across the globe and eventually came to the New World. As domestic cats spread around the world, the species became fully adapted to life with humans.

Chapter Two
The Body Feline

They're the most graceful, sinuous, sexy, truly sensuous creatures in the world.
—Carol Lawrence

The body that nature shaped for the cat over the last 35 million years is an amazing piece of work perfectly designed for hunting, capturing, and digesting prey. The cat's body is fashioned to be a perfect killing machine, although I know it's hard to think of the purring kitty on your lap as a fearsome predator "red in tooth and claw." Many people have difficulty dealing with cats' predatory nature and the behaviors associated with it, such as bringing home limp dead things and leaving them thoughtfully on their owners' pillows. Consequently, some people have trouble understanding feline behavior because they don't fully acknowledge the cat's basic nature. However, it's important to understand that Fluffy is a predator designed to survive by hunting, and much of her behavior is focused on serving this need. This doesn't make her bad—this isn't a good/bad thing—it's just nature's design. A cat hunting in the field for

her supper is no worse than a human who does the same; in fact, from a moral sense, the cat is a good deal better. Unlike humans, cats must eat meat to live.

Of course, cats are also capable of behavior that rises above their predatory nature, just as humans can be more than the sum of their biology. In this chapter the cat's body systems are explored to give you a good feel for the form before we move onto function and behavior.

Feline Anatomy

Mother Nature designed cats to be the ultimate predators, and they cannot walk away from the role nature chose for them any more than we can decide to go back to getting around on all fours. Unlike humans, who can thrive on a vegetarian diet, cats are *obligate carnivores,* which means they must eat meat to survive. The cat's body is designed to hunt that meat, crafted and refined by 35 million years of evolutionary modification (see page 3). The cat's body is exquisitely perfect for the

job, pure poetry in motion. Fundamental grace is a trademark of this species, but in reality the cat is the perfect blend of graceful movement and impressive strength.

The Skeleton

The cat's skeleton, consisting of approximately 244 bones, depending upon the number of bones in the tail, is the structural framework that supports and protects the body's soft tissues. It gives Fluffy stability while providing great flexibility. Cats are designed for maximum speed on all fours, and evolution has modified their skeletons to give extraordinary flexibility plus the ability to climb and sprint. While cats share many design features with other carnivorous mammals, they have design features that make them the efficient hunters they are.

In humans, a rigid collarbone connects the shoulder blades and the breastbone. The collarbone works well as a support between the bones and is useful for carrying heavy loads or supporting the body's

weight, but it also cuts down on the range of motion. This isn't too much of a problem in humans, since we don't ordinarily get around on all fours. In the cat, the collarbone is just a tiny sliver of bone connected to the chest only by muscle. This frees the shoulder blades and allows Fluffy to move her front legs with great freedom, and to lengthen her stride. When you watch Fluffy walk, you can see the tips of her shoulder blades above the spine on either side moving with each step. Combined with a narrow, deep chest, this gives her a long, mobile stride.

The cat's elbows are hinged backward and are ordinarily slightly bent, but when needed, they can be locked in place by the muscles and ligaments around them. The cat's wrists, too, are modified for flexibility, and give her the ability to climb agilely, throw objects in the air, and curl her paws underneath her body when taking a catnap. Bend your palms back flat against your wrists and then lie on them for a few hours and you'll see the design differences

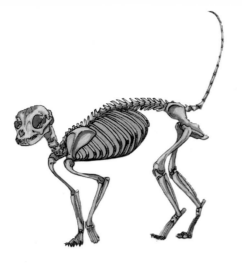

Notice the arrangement of the vertebrae, which allows great flexibility of the spine, and the virtual absence of collarbones, which allows the front limbs to swing freely.

humans do. The foot and hock bones are arranged so that only the front of the foot—the toes and what in humans is called the ball—touches the ground. The digitigrade arrangement is particularly efficient for a hunter that relies on great bursts of speed and agile changes in direction.

The joints are also designed for smooth movement of the limbs and freedom of movement. The ends of the bones are covered with layers of cartilage and are flattened or rounded; this allows the bones to smoothly glide over one another. Each joint is surrounded by a capsule that provides the lubricating *synovial fluid* that creates almost frictionless movement.

The Backbone

When looking at the cat's fluid motion, you may first notice the flexibility of her back. The human backbone provides for flexible movement, but it's rigid compared to the cat's supple spine. It's this willowy central column, and the way the column is attached to the limbs, that allows the cat her athletic motion and her ability to arch her back, perform fluid sprints after prey, and curl up and sleep comfortably in positions that would be agony, or impossible, for a human. The spine consists of 30 vertebrae, not counting the tail. These vertebrae form a long arc that's pliable and allows the cat great freedom of movement. The human backbone contains only 24 vertebrae. Unlike the human backbone, the cat's vertebrae have smooth,

between the wrists of cats and those of humans. It's a rare human who can bend at the wrist like a cat.

There is, however, a downside to this mobility. The muscles and tendons needed to support the flexible legs and joints must be very strong, and this cuts down on the cat's ability to run for long periods. The cat is a sprinter, not a long-distance runner. She uses more energy when moving than, say, the dog; dogs have better endurance in a sustained trot than cats. The cat's hind limbs are not as flexible as the front limbs; they are designed to give strength and power rather than flexible movement.

Cats, like dogs, are *digitigrade,* which means they walk on their toes and the ball of the foot rather than on the entire foot *(plantigrade)* as rounded articulation points that allow the individual vertebra to rotate in almost any direction. This, and the cat's excellent sense of balance, allows her to perform her amazing air-righting maneuver (see Balance, page 18).

The Tail

The tail's vertebrae are called *caudal* vertebrae, and the number of them can vary from cat to cat. Breeds such as the Manx have as few as three, and long-tailed breeds such as the Cornish Rex and the Siamese can have up to 28. The vertebrae in the tail are as flexible as the spine's vertebrae, and help the cat maintain her balance while walking across the top of a fence or a narrow tree branch. The tail is used as a counterweight in the same way a tightrope walker uses the long pole to help maintain balance. Anyone who has tried tightrope walking knows that without a counterweight, it's very difficult, but with a long pole to help maintain your center of gravity, it's a lot easier. The longer the pole, the easier it is to maintain balance, so a longer tail is an advantage. Cats also use their tails for balance when running and executing fine turns. A muscle in the rump region helps control the tail and gives it extra movement options not available to dogs. That's why cats' tails are so expressive.

Short-tailed breeds such as the Manx don't have the advantage of a long tail to help them balance when walking along a narrow object and are therefore at a disadvantage. However, researchers have found that cats born without tails never learn to depend upon them for balance, and they compensate for the lack of a tail. Manx cats are also known to lash their tiny tail stumps when annoyed; it appears that the instinct for this behavior is present even when the tail isn't. Cats that lose their tails in accidents later in life, however, do have balance problems, since they've learned to depend upon their tails. Cats that are declawed suffer from the same sort of problem after the surgery, by the way, often falling off objects because they've come to depend on their claws for traction.

The Teeth

Nature has given the cat an impressive arsenal of defensive and offensive weaponry, namely teeth and claws. Kittens have 26 deciduous "baby" or "milk" teeth. These tiny teeth are as sharp as needles and help the kitten hang onto her mother's nipple. You can tell the

The tail acts as a counterweight to help the cat maintain her balance.

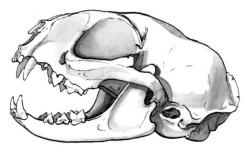

The premolars and molars, called carnassials, work like scissors to cut meat into bite-size pieces. The dagger-like canine teeth in the front are used to hold and kill prey and to rip flesh.

approximate age of a kitten by looking into her mouth; permanent incisors usually appear around four months; permanent canines come in at around six months. These 26 baby teeth eventually fall out just as our baby teeth do and are replaced by 30 adult or permanent teeth at around six months of age. Cats have fewer teeth than both humans and dogs because they are true carnivores—the cat's teeth are designed to bite and tear off hunks of food, and slice and cut the hunks into pieces small enough to swallow. The adult teeth consist of an upper set with six incisors, two canines, six premolars, and two molars, 16 in all. The lower set consists of six incisors, two canines, four premolars, and two molars, 14 in all. The incisors are the tiny teeth directly in front; their purpose is to rip and scrape. The canines, both upper and lower, are used to hold and kill prey, and to tear off hunks of flesh. The molars and premolars cut the meat into bite-size pieces. The lower

molars and the upper premolars at the back work together like shears to cut flesh. These teeth are known as the *carnassials.*

The Claws

The claws are truly amazing in their ability to whip out when required like 18 curved miniature daggers, and retract into a sheath of skin when not needed. This is a truly terrific trait for a predator that needs to stalk its prey on soft, silent feet and then pounce with razor sharp daggers at the end of each finger. Sheathed claws also don't wear down as quickly, keeping the tips nice and sharp for close encounters of the hunting kind. Most cats have 18 claws in all—four on each hind foot and five on each front foot. The fifth claw on each of the front feet is called the dewclaw; it's higher up on the leg and is the feline equivalent of the human thumb.

Polydactyl cats have more than the usual 18 claws; the extra toes are normally on the front feet. Cats have been known to have as many as seven toes on each front foot, and sometimes the number differs between the pair. This is caused by a dominant gene and is therefore hereditary. Polydactyl cats are usually disqualified from being exhibited in shows, but this is purely an aesthetic judgment. The extra toes don't seem to bother the cats or cause them to be less effective hunters. The extra toenails do need to be trimmed regularly, since polydactyl cats have more trouble keeping the extra nails short. Hemingway was known for his collection of polydactyl cats, the descendants of which still live at the Ernest Hemingway Home and Museum in Key West. About half of the 50 cats that currently call the place home are polydactyl.

Claws are not part of the skeleton; a tough, horny protein called *keratin* forms the outer layer of the *epidermis* or *cuticle*. This hard, white, dead cuticle protects the living inner *dermis* or *quick* that contains the nerves and blood supply. The outer cuticle grows constantly from the germinal cells at the end of the terminal bone of the toe, which is one reason why cats scratch. Pulling the extended claws through some rough material helps slough off the worn outer layers of the claws, which exposes the sharp new claw underneath.

The claw is fixed to the terminal toe bone by a fold of skin. Tendons and muscles above and below the toe allow the cat to retract and extend the claws. To extend the claw, the muscles contract, pulling on the tendons. One of the tendons moves the end bone forward, pushing the claw out. Another tendon straightens the toe so the claw can reach its maximum extension. Cats have very good control over their claws and can extend the claws just a little bit—for example, when the mother cat wishes to chastise one of her rambunctious kittens—or fully when the cat really means business—for example, when two rival males battle for territory.

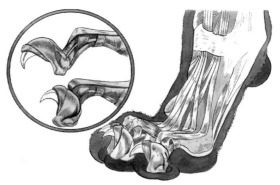

The cat's claws retract when not in use to protect them and keep them sharp. A complex arrangement of ligaments and muscles allows the claws to sheathe and unsheathe.

The Muscles

Of course, the skeleton is merely a framework; it's the muscles that give cats the power they need to sprint after prey or leap on tossed cat toys. The cat's front end is designed for flexibility and support— the guidance system for the engine, in effect—but the hindquarters are the center of power. This power center gives the cat the ability to leap to the top of the bookcase or sprint after a flung toy or a scurrying rodent. If you've ever watched Fluffy go from sitting still to a dead run, you'll notice that she pushes off with her back legs. The powerful muscles of the hind legs work together to give Fluffy her powerful leaping ability, an ability that allows her to leap about five times her own height. A human would have to spring 30 feet (9 m) in the air to match Fluffy's ability to leap.

Movement

Because of their impressive control over their muscles, thanks to their complex nervous system, cats can sprint, climb, turn in the air, stop on a dime, and leap, all with the grace so noted in the species.

When walking, a cat pushes off with her back legs. She moves the legs of one side, and then the legs of the other. The movement of the back leg is followed by the movement of the foreleg; each foot is placed very precisely and cleanly ahead of the one on the other side of the body, so the paw prints of all four feet form an almost straight line. That, combined with her excellent sense of balance, is what allows a cat to walk along the top of a fence or other narrow plank.

When a cat is a bit more hurried, she breaks into a trot. Unlike the walking gait, the trot is *contralateral,* which means the right front leg moves forward with the left hind leg, and the left front leg moves forward with the right hind leg. When Fluffy is *really* in a hurry, she gallops; she pushes off with both hind feet together, allowing for a very strong forward movement. She becomes completely airborne for a split second, hind legs extended behind and front legs extended to the front. The front feet then touch down, one after the other so Fluffy can keep up her momentum. The flexible spine comes into play here, and it helps lengthen the stride by bowing when Fluffy pushes off and straightening when she is airborne. During these gallops a cat can reach up to 30 mph (48 kph); however, a cat can do so for only a short time. Because of their heavy musculature and great flexibility, cats use more energy when they run than a dog does. Cats are sprinters, not long-distance runners. If a short sprint does not gain a cat her intended prey, she will break off and find other prey to pursue.

Jumping

Cats are very good at jumping. They make four basic types of jumps: the impromptu jump, the startle jump, the hunting pounce, and the vertical jump. The impromptu jump is generally seen when a cat is surprised and must make a fast getaway. You can see the impromptu jump when one of your cats unexpectedly leaps at the other. The startle jump occurs when Fluffy is unexpectedly surprised, and all four feet leave the ground simultaneously.

Cats can jump up to five times their own height. Their powerful and marvelously controlled muscles combined with lightning fast reflexes make them agile and graceful.

Cats use the hunting pounce when hunting or catching a toy or the tail of a feline friend; they push off with their back feet and land with the front feet outstretched. The vertical jump is used in scaling the tops of fences, refrigerators, and other hurdles. When Fluffy is leaping onto a surface unknown to her, she carefully estimates the height from the ground, using her excellent depth perception to gauge both height and landing surface. She then crouches and springs, using the back legs to push off. With the front limbs outstretched, Fluffy ascends the height, and touches down with the front legs.

Since cats' claws point backward, climbing down is always more of a problem for them. They must either climb down backward or jump.

Climbing

Cats are excellent climbers, and they appear to enjoy climbing just for the fun of it. They also use this ability in both hunting and escaping enemies. A cat begins her climb with a powerful leap, using the strong muscles of the back legs to hoist herself aloft and the front and rear claws to grip. The front legs are also used to hug the object for control and balance. The claws work like crampons, in which spikes are attached to shoes to give traction, to dig in and hoist the cat upward.

Coming down is more of a problem for the cat. The claws, since they curve backward, are no help in a face-first descent, and the powerful back legs only speed the descent. This means that she must either back down, which is awkward since she can't see where she's going, or come down front first with no way of braking. Cats generally jump outward away from the tree as soon as possible to lessen the impact on the front feet. Sometimes, Fluffy cannot make the descent on her own, and becomes trapped in a tree or on a pole; her excellent depth perception is then a disadvantage. She can see how far it is down to the ground, becomes frightened, and can remain stuck until rescued.

Slinking and Crouching

Cats have the ability to quickly sprint after prey, but they also can slink stealthily and crouch motionlessly for long periods. They are able to do this due to *slow-twitch* muscle fibers that produce slow sustained contractions and resist fatigue. These slow-twitch fibers allow cats to hold positions that would quickly become agony for a human. This ability is important when Fluffy is stalking prey because one of the strategies she uses is to lie in wait, pouncing when the prey comes near. She also needs these slow-twitch fibers when she is, for example, creeping stealthily through the grass so she can get close to her prey before she uses her hunting pounce.

Balance

Fluffy has a very good sense of balance that allows her to run across the top of a fence, balance on the limb of a tree, and right herself when falling. This is due to the construction of the inner ear, which is responsible for body orientation and balance. The *vestibular apparatus* in the inner ear sends information to the cat's brain regarding the body's position, which then directs her movements. The apparatus is made up of semicircular fluid-filled canals arranged at right angles to each other to detect movement in any direction. These canals are lined with millions of tiny hairs connected to flaps of tissue. When the cat moves, the fluid in the canals moves and disturbs the flaps of tissue and their tiny hairs, sending directional information to the brain.

Self-righting Reflex

It is the vestibular apparatus, plus the cat's flexible spine, that allows her to right herself when falling. When a cat falls with her feet higher than her body, the self-righting reflex takes over. She first aligns her head and then twists her front end 180 degrees so the front feet face the ground. Finally, she twists her back legs around so she can land on her feet, minimizing injury. She is able to do this in the time it takes to drop approximately 2 feet (61 cm). As she lands, her back arches to minimize the force of the fall. Her legs relax and act as shock absorbers.

How many humans do you know who could fall from the top of a high-rise and survive? It would be a miracle for a human to survive such a fall, but in New York City, a cat fell out of an apartment window, plummeted 32 stories, and walked away with only a broken tooth. This is not to say cats always land on their feet, but their righting reflex and efficient vestibular apparatus certainly help lessen possible damage.

You might be tempted to test this righting ability on Fluffy at home, but please don't. Your cat could sustain injuries from even a short fall. She needs the time and room in which to perform the self-righting reflex. Cats have gained a reputation for being indestructible and always landing on their feet, but that's not so. Cats can miscalculate; they can even be clumsy on occasion. So don't take chances with Fluffy's life; just take my word for it—your cat does have the self-righting reflex.

The Animal Medical Center in New York City conducted a study on "high-rise syndrome," the name given for injuries sustained when an animal falls from a substantial height. The study included 132 cats that had experienced such falls. Researchers found that cats that fell four stories or less, and ten stories or more, tended to have the fewest injuries. The cats that fell between five and nine stories were often the most seriously injured. The reason that a cat falling a longer distance would receive fewer severe injuries is due to the effect of "free-fall" on a cat. When a cat reaches terminal velocity, the point where the cat's rate of acceleration stops and the rate of travel stays constant, the acceleration no longer stimulates the vestibular apparatus, and the cat relaxes. A cat is less likely to sustain damage when she hits the ground in a relaxed state.

The Brain

Of course, the cat's magnificent body would be nothing without her remarkable brain, which is the command center of the body. Fluffy's ratio of brain weight to body weight is greater than in most mammals other than simians and humans, which indicates that the potential for intelligence is high. Her cerebral hemispheres are large and convoluted, and this is typical of intelligent animals. The brain is protected not only by the tough skull bones but also by fluid and a three-layered membrane called the *meninges.*

The brain consists of three main parts: the *cerebellum,* the *cerebrum,* and the *brain stem.* The cerebellum controls the cat's balance and movement. This part of the brain is highly developed and large, and combined with the cat's graceful, fluid body, allows her to react with lightning speed.

The cerebrum is the largest of the three parts, and is the section of the brain that coordinates the input received by the cat's sensory receptors and her muscles. The cerebrum is divided into two cerebral hemispheres consisting of four lobes: frontal, parietal, occipital, and temporal. The frontal lobe is related to movement, voluntary control of fine motor skills, and learning and other intellectual activities. The parietal lobe is associated with touch, pain,

Cats stretch upon awakening to restore circulation and flex muscles.

and the perception of temperature. The occipital lobe deciphers visual information. The temporal lobe is associated with memory and behavior; it also interprets information brought to the brain by the cat's ears. Each cerebral hemisphere possesses a relatively large olfactory bulb that deals with the sense of smell, not surprising since this sense plays such an important role in Fluffy's life.

The brain stem is the central core of the brain and houses the *hypothalamus,* the *pituitary gland,* and the *reticular formation.* The hypothalamus controls basic instincts such as aggression, fear, hunger, and sexual and maternal behavior. The pituitary gland is linked to and controlled by the hypothalamus; by releasing pituitary hormones, the hypothalamus controls the cat's behavior. The reticular formation keeps the brain awake and alert and switches off during sleep.

The brain receives and sends messages via the nerves. The nerves or *neurons* are the building blocks of the nervous system and transport information from all around the body. Each nerve is composed of a cell body that contains the nucleus and the surrounding cytoplasm, short branchlike structures called *dendrites,* and extended "fingers" called *axons.* The dendrites receive messages from other nerves. Axons transmit neurons and send out electrical impulses from the nerve cell body to other nerves or organs in the body. Each axon ends in thousands of "terminals." Each terminal is capable of sending messages to other neurons. While the axons of the neurons never actually touch the neurons they communicate with, they send their messages by releasing chemical messengers called neurotransmitters into the synaptic cleft, the gap between the neurons. Neurotransmitters navigate the synaptic cleft and attach to receptors on the receiving neuron. At any moment of the day, literally billions of such messages are being sent.

Chapter Three
The Cat's Senses

It always gives me a shiver when I see a cat seeing what I can't see.
—Eleanor Farjeon

To be able to have an affectionate relationship with your cat, you first must have an understanding of how Tiger perceives the world around him. In the last chapter, you learned how the cat's body works. In this chapter, we'll explore Tiger's five senses—six if you count the feline's mysterious "sixth sense." These senses gather data about the environment and transmit these data to the brain, where they are processed into usable information.

Hearing

Since the cat has survived millennia by hunting prey animals, the sense of hearing is very important to its survival. Tiger's hearing is ultrasensitive; not only can he hear sounds too faint for our ears, such as the rustlings of a mouse, he can also hear sounds higher in pitch than we can perceive. His hearing is "tuned" to a higher frequency because the sounds of his usual prey—rodents, small mammals, and birds—are usually high pitched. This sensitivity is also important when a mother cat is raising her young, since kittens also make higher-pitched sounds.

Cats hear at least 1½ octaves above the limit of human hearing, so they even exceed dogs' renowned ability to hear high-pitched sounds. This is the reason that cats respond to higher-pitched voices, and the reason many cat owners talk to their cats in higher-pitched tones. Cats respond more readily to the higher frequencies.

The cat's superior hearing may also explain the phenomenon sometimes called "seeing Martians," in which Tiger, relaxing happily in your lap, suddenly raises his head and stares wide-eyed at the wall over your shoulder, giving you the creepy feeling that some invisible creature is standing just behind you when you can't see or hear a thing. That doesn't mean that there's nothing to hear, however. Your cat has just

More than a dozen muscles enable the cat's ears to swivel toward the source of sounds.

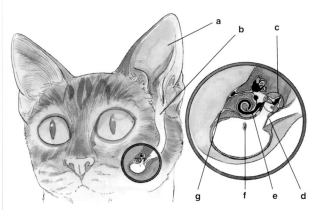

(a) The pinna or ear flap, (b) external auditory canal, (c) the hammer, (d) ear drum, anvil and stirrup, called the ear ossicles, (e) cochlea, (f)auditory nerve leading to the brain, (g) internal auditory canals.

detected some interesting sound too faint or high pitched for your hearing.

Sounds are vibrations—pressure waves—that are transmitted through the air. Pitch depends on the frequency of the waves and the amplitude or size of the waves. The higher the sound, the faster the wave; the louder the sound, the larger the wave. The ear flap, or *pinna,* serves to funnel these vibrations down the external auditory canal to the eardrum. Three bones called the *ossicles* then transfer the sound vibration to the snail-shaped *cochlea* in the inner ear, which differentiates between the frequencies and amplitudes of various sounds and converts the sounds to electrical impulses. The auditory nerve then carries these impulses to the brain, where they are translated as sounds.

Not only is Tiger's hearing acute, his ears are equipped with more than a dozen muscles that enable him to swivel 180 degrees toward the source of sounds. When you see Tiger sitting with his back to you but with his ears furled backward, this means that, although he appears to be ignoring you, he is keeping an ear on your movements. This aural arrangement helps funnel the sounds to the cochlea and also makes it easier to locate the source of the sounds extremely accurately, which is important when your dinner is a minuscule mouse. These ear muscles also allow Tiger to flatten his ears when faced with combat, reducing the chance of injury to the sensitive pinna.

Sight

If you think Tiger's ears are extraordinary, wait until you hear about his eyes. The feline's sense of sight is highly developed and allows him to see in almost total darkness as well as in the brightest sunlight. Although cats cannot, as you may have heard, see in total darkness—no creature can except those that produce their own light sources—cats' eyes use the available light much more efficiently than ours do. This is due in part to the *tapetum lucidum,* a reflective layer of cells that line the back of the retina. This "mirror of the eye" reflects unused light back through the retina, giving the light-sensitive retinal cells a second chance to use the light. The tapetum lucidum is the reason that Tiger's eyes appear to glow when caught in a beam of light such as a car's headlights. Most nocturnal animals possess this set of specialized cells.

Proportionally, cats' eyes are much larger in relation to their body size than ours are. In addition, cats are able to dilate their pupils to fill almost all of the visible portion of the eyes. This allows even dim light to reach the cat's retina. Tiger's eyes also dilate when he feels threatened, allowing him to better see the threat. Cats are able to close their pupils to a small vertical slit, protecting the sensitive retina from intense light. This slit is more efficient at protecting the eye than our round pupils.

Since cats are predators, their eyes are positioned close together

Cats, like most nocturnal animals, have a mirror-like layer of cells on the back of the retina that makes their eyes glow when caught in a beam of light.

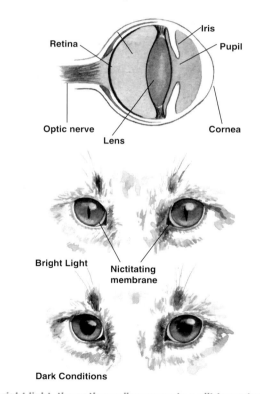

Bright Light

Nictitating membrane

Dark Conditions

In bright light, the cat's pupil narrows to a slit to protect the eye. In near darkness, the cat's pupil dilates until it is almost round to collect all available light. The nictitating membrane, also known as the third eyelid or haw, is a thin layer of skin that closes diagonally across the eye under the eyelid. It protects and lubricates the cornea.

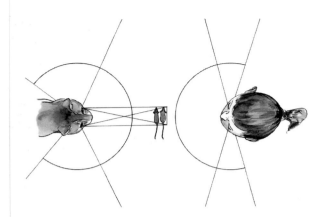

The cat's binocular vision allows the cat to see in three dimensions. Each eye sends a slightly different viewpoint of the mouse back to the brain, which the brain compares to judge size, distance, and depth. The cat's total field of vision is 285 degrees compared to our 210 degrees.

Because their corneas are larger in relation to the size of the cat's eyes and are more curved than ours, the cat's total field of vision is wider than ours—285 degrees to our 210 degrees. When Tiger is looking directly ahead, he can see movement in any direction except directly behind him. This wide area of peripheral vision is highly tuned to movement, so even when it appears Tiger doesn't notice you, he likely is very much aware of your presence. He just isn't acknowledging you at the moment, as cats are apt to do.

Because the eye's lens, which performs fine adjustments to the focusing of retinal images, is controlled by comparatively weak muscles, cats cannot focus very well on close objects. A cat sees best at a range of about 7 to 20 feet (2.1 to 6.1 m).

Recognizing Colors

In recognizing colors, cats are also not very adept. Where we can distinguish between minute color variations, cats can see only a few colors. When light hits the retina, chemical reactions occur in millions of specialized receptor cells called *rods* and *cones,* each named for its shape. The rods do not perceive color; they perceive only the light and dark tones of an image, and can distinguish outlines or silhouettes of objects in almost complete darkness. Cats have a greater number of rods in relation to the number of cones—about twenty-five to one—whereas in humans the ratio is about

at the front of the head, unlike prey animals such as rabbits and mice, whose eyes are placed wide apart on the sides of the head for maximum detection of predators. Predators such as cats need this frontal visual arrangement to give them the proper field of vision for hunting prey. The field of vision of each eye partially overlaps the other; this is called *binocular vision.* The cat has approximately 130 degrees of binocular vision as opposed to humans' 120 degrees. When Tiger looks at his prey, each eye sends a slightly different view to the brain. The brain interprets these two views into a three-dimensional image, which allows Tiger to accurately judge the distance between him and his potential prey, crucial data for a successful hunter.

four to one in favor of the rods. The large number of rods helps Tiger to see in near darkness. For a nocturnal predator, this kind of adaptation is vital to survival.

The cones detect the fine lines and points of an image. Humans have three types of cones; each absorbs light in certain wavelengths (blue-violet, green, and yellow and red), allowing us to see a wide range of colors. For many years, scientists thought that cats could see only in monochrome because they could not successfully train cats to distinguish between colors, but cats were later successfully trained to distinguish red, blue, and white from one another. Green- and blue-sensitive cones have been found in the feline eye, but not red-sensitive cones, which probably means that to a cat red appears dark gray.

The extreme difficulty of training cats to distinguish between colors—cats seem to have a hard time understanding the point of doing so—tells us that color perception is not highly developed, likely because it is unimportant to feline survival. Seeing in dim light and detecting movement is much more important than, say, being able to tell if the intended prey is a red bird or a blue one. For omnivores like us, color distinction is much more important for our survival in an evolutionary sense; being able to detect the ripeness of fruit or distinguishing between edible and poisonous varieties of fungi requires keen color perception. Therefore, the color of

The cat's whiskers are long, stiff hairs that are extremely touch-sensitive.

the cat bed you buy is most likely lost on your feline friend; you should consider your own tastes in such matters. Tiger will only care about how comfortable the bed is.

Touch

This brings us to the next sense—touch. Certain areas of the cat's body are highly sensitive and vital to his hunting ability. Touch is also important in many other ways: Kittens, born blind and deaf, find their way to their mother's nipple for their first meal by using their sense of touch. The sense of touch provides Tiger with vital information regarding pressure, warmth, cold, and, of course, pain. This information is transmitted to the brain, where it is processed so Tiger can take the proper action—crawling out from under his heavy littermate, moving away from a too-hot fire, finding a warm place to sleep, and fleeing when you step on his tail.

The cat's whiskers are important touch receptors. Twice as thick as guard hairs and extending three times deeper into the skin, these touch-sensitive *vibrissae* are so significant that in the womb they are the first hairs to develop. While you probably are most familiar with the long whiskers that grow from the whiskers pads under and on each side of the nose, cats actually have four types of whisker tufts on the face:

1. *Mystacial* that grow from the whisker pads

2. *Genal* that grow from the outer corners of the eyes

3. *Superciliary* that grow above the eyes

4. *Mandibular* that grow on the chin.

Cats also have tufts of whiskers growing from the back of each front leg just above the carpal pad.

The follicles of these hairs extend deeper into the dermis, or lower skin layer. Each whisker root is surrounded by a fibrous, blood-filled capsule and is joined by a network of sensory nerves. Because of this construction, the whiskers are highly sensitive and provide Tiger with a great deal of information. Even air currents can be detected by this feline radar. The slightest movement of the whiskers stimulates the network of nerves and provides detailed information about the cat's environment. This is vital to Tiger's ability to move about with confidence at night. This sensory system allows him to creep through thick bushes and cluttered barns and storerooms, virtually by feel, and avoid injury. Cats may use their whiskers to tell if they can fit through a tight space because the whiskers are usually about the width of the cat's body.

Also, the whiskers play an important role in hunting. Since cats' near vision is poor, the sensitive whiskers take over when Tiger pounces on his prey. The whiskers on the back of the forelegs help him feel the struggling quarry, which helps detect and foil any escape attempts, and the facial whiskers help him deliver the killing bite to the neck with precision.

Each whisker is equipped with *arrector muscles* that allow voluntary

Cats use their whiskers to gauge the width of narrow openings.

movement as well. Cats generally move their whiskers forward when greeting their human or animal friends, and backward for protection when eating or fighting. Because the whiskers are so sensitive, some cats do not like to have them touched, while others enjoy having their whiskers smoothed back by a gentle human hand. Your cat will let you know which he prefers. The sensitivity of the whiskers may also explain why some cats avoid eating and drinking from small, deep bowls; the rim of the bowl may touch the whiskers and distract Tiger from enjoying his meal.

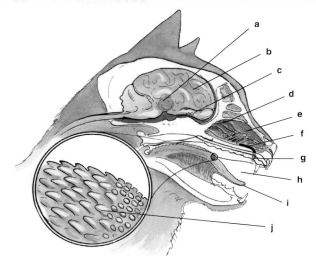

(a) Hypothalamus, (b) brain, (c) olfactory lobe, (d) olfactory mucosa, (e) nasal cavities, (f) Jacobson's organ, (g) duct leading from the mouth to the Jacobson's organ, (h) the mouth, (i) tongue, (j) papillae.

Smell and Taste

Although the dog's olfactory sense is far better than the cat's, and worlds better than ours, cats have a finely tuned sense of smell that they use not only to gather information but also as a means of communication. We humans primarily use our senses of sight and hearing to gather information about our world; only if deprived of sight do we learn to use our sense of smell as a primary means of gathering information. We principally think of smells in terms of what we like and dislike rather than as sources of data, and even go out of our way to eliminate or disguise our natural odors. Cats, however, use their senses of smell and taste, as well as their senses of hearing and sight, to perceive and define their environment. The cat's

sense of smell is nearly four times better than ours. They probably use their senses of smell and taste to recognize and define their world the way we use our highly developed color sense to recognize environmental landmarks. With our weak sense of smell, we can only imagine the rich world of aromas perceived by our feline companions.

Smell and its companion sense, taste, team up to become a sensory system known as the *chemical senses.* Smell and taste organs are closely linked; both senses are registered in the same part of the brain, and the nasal passage opens into the mouth. This sensory system allows the cat to gather information and transmit that information to the brain.

Smell

When a cat breathes in through the nose, air enters the nostrils and passes through into a maze of nasal cavities. Each cavity contains three small, folded bones called *turbinates,* which provide a greater surface area to filter, warm, and humidify the inhaled air before it enters the lungs. The turbinates are covered with a sticky membrane rich in blood vessels and specialized nerve cells called the *olfactory mucosa.* The olfactory mucosa is comparatively quite large—3 to 6 square inches (19 to 38 cm²)—which is nearly twice the size of the olfactory mucosa in humans. Yet, we possess the same olfactory setup. The cat's olfactory nerve cells, all 200 million of them, are highly sensitive to the gaseous odors that enter when the cat breathes in. The cells send information about the odors to the *olfactory bulbs,* which are directly linked to the brain.

The first sense to develop—cats are born both blind and deaf; these senses activate four to ten days after birth—the sense of smell guides kittens to their first food, their mother's milk. The kittens then use their sense of smell to find their way back to the same nipple for each feeding, and to find their mother if they wander a short distance away from her side. As kittens grow and become able to see and hear, they still use their sense of smell for a wide variety of functions, such as recognizing friends and foes, finding receptive mates, perceiving danger, identifying the territories of other cats, and marking their own domain (see Olfactory Language, page 63).

Taste

Tiger's tongue, long and dexterous with an abrasive surface, serves several purposes involved with eating, catching prey, and grooming. Because of the variety of functions, the tongue possesses a great array of sensory receptors; however, the cat has relatively few taste buds— 473 compared to our 9,000. Because of this, the smell of Tiger's food will determine to a great extent his enjoyment of the meal. That's the reason cats enjoy their food warm; the aroma is released by the heat. Cats that lose their sense of smell usually lose their appetites and must be encouraged to eat.

The feline tongue is covered by numerous knobs called *papillae,* of which there are several types. Those in the tongue's center, *filiform papillae,* form backward-pointing hooks that remove loose fur while Tiger is grooming, rasp meat from bones while he is eating, and collect water when he is drinking. These papillae have no taste receptors. The taste receptors are carried on mushroom-shaped papillae, *fungiform papillae,* along the front and side edges of the tongue, and on the four to six large cup-shaped papillae, *vallate papillae,* at the back of the tongue.

Cats have taste buds that respond to salt, sour, and bitter tastes, but have few that respond to the taste of sweets. Cats are sensitive to the taste of water, and it appears that the taste buds responsive to the taste of water are also those that are responsive to sweets. Protein-based tastes seem to activate the taste buds, but fats seem to be registered as smells rather than tastes. This means that a preference of one kind of meat over another is largely a difference in scent rather than taste.

The Flehmen Response

Cats can smell by breathing through either the nose or the mouth, because the nasal passage opens into the mouth. They have a sense that we lack and that can best be described as a cross between taste and smell. This sense is governed by the *Jacobson's* or *vomeronasal* organ situated between the nose and the palate; it is connected to the roof of the mouth by a duct located behind the upper incisor teeth. The organ is rich in olfactory cells, as is the olfactory mucosa. Cats access this organ by the *flehmen response.* When they smell something interesting, they open their mouths in a distinctive slack-jawed grimace that helps bring the odors into the mouth and in contact with the vomeronasal organ. The organ gathers tiny chemical molecules from the odors, the data from which it transmits directly to the brain.

Although the purpose of this organ is not completely understood, many studies have been done on the flehmen response and researchers believe that its primary purpose is to collect sexual information. Unneutered toms seeking in-heat queens are the most enthusiastic flehmers, and will flehm in response to the smell of the queen's urine, which informs them of her sexual readiness. However, neutered cats of both sexes have been known to flehm, not only in response to feline odors but also in reaction to the smell of catnip and other odors. It appears that cats use the response to savor particularly interesting smells.

The Cat's "Sixth Sense"

Imagine yourself blindfolded, driven around in circles, and dumped in an unfamiliar area with no street signs or friendly people to ask for help. Would you be able to shake yourself off, turn around, and march straight for home? Probably not. However, it appears that cats can. Although some researchers doubt the existence of this ability, many believe there is ample evidence that cats have an as-yet unidentified sense that allows them to find their way home, sometimes over distances of hundreds of miles and across such barriers as rivers and cities. Many reliable accounts of these amazing journeys exist.

No one really knows how cats accomplish this feat, but cat researchers have proposed certain theories. One favored theory is that cats use the position of the sun and

Some people believe that a mysterious sixth sense allows cats to find their way home from great distances. Others believe that cats accomplish these feats by efficient use of their five senses.

the earth's magnetic fields to negotiate their way back to familiar territory. Minute iron deposits in the cat's body act like built-in compasses to give him a sense of direction that humans lack or have forgotten how to use. When closer to home, cats use their keen senses of smell and hearing, as well as sight, to find their home turf.

This sensitivity to the earth's magnetic fields may also explain why some cats—and dogs—seem able to predict earthquakes. Hours, or even days, before an earthquake, some cats know something is about to happen and act disoriented and frightened, and sometimes even flee for safer territory.

Jim Berkland, a California geologist, accurately predicted the 1989 San Francisco Bay Area earthquake and the 1994 southern California Northridge quake. How? By scanning the "lost pet" ads. He had found that the number of missing pet ads rises dramatically a day or two before an earthquake. According to Berkland, the magnetic field fluctuates before the quake actually occurs, and cats are so sensitive to these changes that they attempt to escape the coming danger.

Of course, this "sensitivity to the earth's magnetic field" theory doesn't explain the mysterious stories of cats that, left behind when their owners move, somehow find their way to their owners' new homes, places where they have never been. The earth's magnetic field or the position of the sun would be no help there. This ability is referred to as *psi-trailing,* suggesting that cats perform this feat by using psychic powers. However, some have suggested that cats, with their keen sense of smell, are able to locate their owners just by following their owners' scent. If true, that feat is just about as incredible as the use of telepathy would be.

Cats appear to be sensitive to other planetary changes as well. Japanese fishermen and sailors have known for centuries that one can predict the weather by watching cats. Sailors even took cats to sea with them for their ability to predict storms. One theory explaining this weather-predicting ability contends that cats can sense changes in barometric pressure. Another theory maintains that cats can smell far-off rain. Still another says that cats pick up changes in the bioelectric field or shifts in the ionization. Whatever the reason, cats have developed a reputation as the forecasters of the animal kingdom.

That cats are known for their extrasensory perceptions is really not as much of a mystery as it appears. Cats are predators; their bodies are finely tuned hunting instruments programmed to detect minute variations in their environment. Curious, smart, and ever-watchful, cats use their intelligence and ability to problem-solve in order to survive on a hostile planet. For that reason, cats, big and small, are among the most efficient predators the world has ever known.

Chapter Four

The Cat's Mind

We cannot, without becoming cats, perfectly understand the cat mind.

—St. George Mivart

The Sensitive Period

Some behaviors seem hardwired into Fluffy's makeup from the start; others are learned as she grows and gains experiences from her environment. A cat's behavior is a combination of these innate skills and learned behaviors—nature and nurture determine a cat's actions. Essentially, cats have an innate set of qualities, but the manner in which these traits are expressed is shaped by the cat's early experiences.

Cats, like many animals, have a period in which behaviors begin to manifest themselves and during which they are sensitive to external experiences that will affect their behavior for life. This *sensitive period* lasts from about two to five weeks of age, and is the most critical period in Fluffy's development and socialization. During this period, she begins

to exhibit genetically programmed behaviors that come into play at certain stages of her development. These behaviors include activities such as grooming; at a certain age cats begin to groom themselves without any prompting. Hunting is another innate behavior; all cats have the inborn instinct to hunt prey.

During the sensitive period Fluffy becomes socialized to members of her own species and to other species as well, such as humans. Cats that don't get the proper socialization during this period generally have social problems as adults.

How Cats Learn

Cats use observation and imitation to learn; in fact, one of the signs of cat intelligence is their ability to learn by watching the actions of others. Cats can and do learn from watching cats that are unrelated to them, but they learn more quickly and willingly from their mothers. For example, how well Mother teaches her kittens hunting skills determines how effective the kittens will be as hunters. Since being a good hunter is important for survival in the wild, it's not surprising that domestic cats have the instinct to learn these skills as well as to pass them onto their offspring.

Cats also seem very good at figuring things out for themselves and learning by observation and trial and error. For example, Punkin, my Abyssinian, was in my office one day, bored since I was working, and looking for amusement. Idly, she began swatting at the fragile knick-knacks on the shelf beside my desk. I picked her up and, to distract her from breaking my trinkets, took her into the kitchen for a treat. Cats learn very quickly—now she knows that the way to get a treat is to charge into my office and bat knick-knacks off the shelf. It works every time. But by using the same reward system, we can train our cats to do things that we really want them to do, instead of reinforcing naughty behavior we'd just as soon avoid.

Play

While play makes cats and kittens fun companions, all the rolling around on the floor and playful leaping has a vital role in cat development. The young of most mammals play, and it is interesting to note that the most intelligent species such as carnivores, dolphins, apes, monkeys, and so on, are the most playful species. The role of play in development is really not fully understood, but it's clear that it has an important

Mother cats prepare their kittens for adulthood by teaching them basic survival skills such as hunting.

developmental role. Kittens learn important social and hunting skills that they'll need later in life during their early sessions of play. You'll notice that during play, kittens practice their developing hunting skills. To encourage cats—and people—to play, the brain releases chemicals called *enkephalins* that stimulate the brain's pleasure centers. Kittens raised in isolation will have significant social problems and be very poor hunters, and it's thought that this is due to the lack of opportunities to play.

Play also has many benefits for adult cats. It helps keep cats healthy, since the strenuous physical activities performed strengthen the muscles, stimulate the muscles, lungs, and heart, increase flexibility and coordination, and help lessen obesity. Play also keeps Fluffy mentally alert and helps combat boredom and depression, particularly for indoor-only cats.

During play, kittens learn important social skills and hunting techniques.

Lastly, participating in Fluffy's play can strengthen your bond with her (see page 72).

Early Socialization

Early socialization is important if cats are to become well-adjusted adults. Human interaction is vital during the sensitive period when the cat is like a blank computer disk, ready to download everything she experiences during that time. In order for a cat to be truly comfortable around humans, she must have human contact—hands-on contact. Without handling, kittens may never learn to fully trust humans and may never truly accept them as members of their family. When acquiring a kitten you must make sure she has had enough of the right kind of handling or your chances of bonding with her will be slim.

Cats also need contact with their mothers and with other cats. Cats taken away from their mothers too early have problems later on. Poorly socialized cats, untutored in the survival skills, are usually poor hunters. All cats have the instinct to chase small, scurrying rodents, but without instruction they do not learn to deliver the killing bite to the back of the neck. For a house cat, this is no great loss, since you most likely won't want Fluffy bringing home prey; however, mother cats teach not only hunting skills but also social skills. A cat's lack of social skills can affect her relationship with humans, too. For example, cats that lack proper upbringing can bite too hard or scratch when playing because they didn't learn to pull their punches when they were kittens.

One theory about why socialization is so important is that stimulation affects the functioning of the adrenal and pituitary glands and the parts of the brain responsible for reacting to stress. More stimulation makes a cat better able to cope with new or stressful events; therefore she is less fearful of new situations.

Clancy, the newest member of our cat family, rescued after some thoughtless person dumped him off in the park across the street, is an example of a cat taken away from his mother too young. Since he didn't get enough early instruction on how cats behave around each other, he flounces up to the other cats and playfully leaps on them, knocking them down, and is hurt and puzzled when they react with hisses, growls, and swats across the face. He just wants to play. He'll then sadly come and sit beside me and, while kneading me with one paw, nurse on his own belly. Apparently, his mother's nipples weren't available to him for long enough so he came up with this novel way to comfort himself.

He's also frightened of anything new. Strangers panic him, so much so that when we merely change into different clothes, he runs from us in terror.

To avoid such behavior problems, you should allow cats to stay with their mothers for their first 12 weeks, longer if possible. Human socialization is vital in raising well-socialized cats, but it cannot replace maternal attention. Resist the urge to take your kitten home at eight weeks; kittens are indeed cute at that age, but they need time with their mothers in order to become well-socialized members of feline—and human—society.

Early handling is important if your cat is to become a well-socialized adult.

The Hunting Instinct

Cats are predators and have an instinctive desire to hunt. When Fluffy leaps on your toes or stalks a cat toy, she is practicing hunting skills. While not all cats learn to be good hunters, they all have the instinctual desire. Hunger doesn't trigger the hunting instinct, so making cats go hungry won't turn them into better mousers. In fact, studies show that well-nourished cats make better hunters than undernourished ones. Commonly, cats' prey consists of mice, rats, and other rodents, and small ground-dwelling mammals such as squirrels and rabbits. Cats are opportunistic hunters, however, and will also eat fish, lizards, frogs,

Play serves to hone the hunting skills.

insects, and other small prey when the opportunity presents itself.

Cats also eat birds, but studies indicate that birds comprise no more than 10 percent of the feline diet. Some people blame cats for the reduction in the populations of song birds, but research shows that cats have little impact on most bird populations. Unfortunately, the major culprit is humankind; the destruction of bird habitat and pesticides are the major causes of the decline.

Cats habitually hunt at night when their primary prey is active. That's why Fluffy races around when you're trying to sleep. When hunting, she conceals herself in a place that gives her a good view of the hunting area; for example, she might crouch in a stand of tall grass or at the base of a wall. When she sights prey, she crouches low. Her eyes dilate. She creeps forward very slowly and silently, pausing often to watch her intended prey. Only the tip of the tail twitches to show her excitement. She prepares to pounce by tensing, shifting weight to her toes, and treading with her back feet. Finally, she springs, pinning the prey with her front feet, and delivers the death bite to the nape of the neck.

Sometimes a cat won't kill her prey immediately, but will play with it, releasing and recapturing the prey repeatedly. While this strikes us as unduly cruel, researchers believe this behavior, like play, serves to hone the hunting skills. It also may serve to tire the prey so that the cat will not be injured when delivering the final bite. Some researchers speculate that this behavior arises from a lack of hunting skills. A cat that doesn't learn from the mother how to deliver the killing bite will continue to toy with the prey, not knowing how to end it. If you find this behavior upsetting, it might be comforting to know that a number of studies have been done on prey animals, and the animals may not suffer as much as we might think. An animal caught by a predator exhibits the "defeated mouse" syndrome, where the body floods with endorphins, masking pain and producing sedation and euphoria. An animal in that state is likely not to suffer much.

If Fluffy's predatory nature disturbs you, keep her indoors. She will practice her hunting skills on her favorite cat toy and be safer for it. And remember that predators play an essential role in maintaining the earth's ecological balance. Without predators to control the numbers, the populations of prey species would rise. They would soon find themselves short of food and would fall victim to starvation and disease from overcrowding. Predators keep prey species healthy, too; culling the weak, sick, and slow members of a species causes the species to become stronger. The strong, healthy members of the species are then able to reproduce themselves and pass along their strength and health to future generations. Both predators and prey are needed to protect the delicate balance of nature. Where this system fails, inevitably, is where humankind has interfered with nature's balance. The near extinction of the cat species has caused serious repercussions in many animal populations.

Hunting is natural behavior for cats; they will hunt even when well fed.

Bringing Home Prey

A cat that is allowed outside may bring home prey and proudly present it to you or leave it as a gift on your pillow. This means that Fluffy accepts you as a family member. She brings you the prey so that you can learn how to hunt; carrying prey home for the kittens' education is normal behavior. Fluffy thinks she's teaching you by giving you an example by which to learn. Cats probably think we're terribly slow learners.

Keeping Fluffy inside will solve this problem. She will use toys to satisfy the urge to hunt. If she gets out and brings home prey, or catches prey inside your home,

rather than recoil with distaste or scold her, accept the gift and profusely praise her cunning and skill. Remember, bringing home prey means she thinks of you as part of her family; don't punish her for her loyalty. Then quietly dispose of the token as soon as possible because rodents and birds can harbor infectious diseases and parasites.

Covering Tracks

Another hunting-related behavior can be observed at dinnertime. When Fluffy has finished eating, she scratches around her bowl as if trying to bury the leftovers. This is not a comment on the cuisine, nor is it related to the habit of covering urine and feces, although the same reason lies behind both actions. Cats bury their wastes and their leftovers to cover their scent and keep bigger predators or dominant members of their species from tracking them.

Instinctively, cats bury their wastes and leftovers to prevent attracting the attention of larger predators.

The Cat's Social Life

Cats are social animals. The myth that cats are solitary and therefore incapable of true affection has haunted felines for years, possibly because cats are solitary hunters and territorial animals, and, because of that, humans have made the error of thinking cats don't need companionship. Unlike dogs, cats have no instinctual need to cooperate in packs. Cats defend their territory from intruders, and therefore often seem aloof and independent. That is not to say they cannot feel affection toward other animals and humans. When given a chance, cats will meet you halfway.

Cats are territorial by nature, and their society is structured in a dominance-controlled hierarchy governed by strict rules of conduct. In the wild, each cat has an area called the *core territory* or *home base,* which is that

cat's alone and which she will defend from intruders. This area is relatively small, and the size and location depend upon the cat's order in the hierarchy. Each cat also has a larger area called the *home range* where she hunts and explores. This area usually overlaps the home ranges of other cats. The size of these areas depends upon the shelter provided and the abundance of food. If food is plentiful, many cats may live peaceably in a relatively small area. If food is hard to come by or the source is unreliable, a single cat may have a home range of as much as 100 acres (40 ha). As you may have guessed, these territorial instincts are motivated by survival instincts; a cat must have an area in which she can hunt unchallenged by other cats competing for the same food source.

Cats take turns using the common areas within their ranges. They will announce their presence in the area by scent marking, thereby avoiding confrontations with other cats that might lead to fighting and injury. When a cat enters the shared area and finds signs that another cat is present, that cat will usually leave and come back later. As the cats learn each other's routines, they tend to visit certain areas at set times when other cats are not present. Cats have an excellent time sense and use it to avoid confrontations. With this "time-sharing" arrangement cats can avoid fighting.

Males in a feline community fight to determine their order in the dominance hierarchy. When a new cat arrives in the territory, he must fight the established toms to confirm his place in the social structure. The results of these fights are generally final. Once the new cat establishes his rank, he doesn't have to fight again unless he's challenged for his place, he challenges a higher-ranking tom's position, or he participates in challenging a newcomer to the area. (Males also fight for female cats in heat.) The top-ranking tomcat controls the largest territory, but since he knows he's the top cat, he may allow intruders to pass through his territory unchallenged, as long as they do not try to linger too long. When he does choose to fight, however, he usually wins.

Males and Females

Males and females generally do not spend time together except

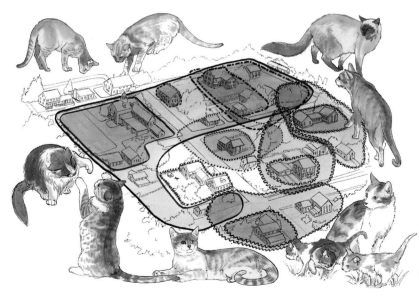

Home ranges usually overlap, while core territories belong only to the owners. The territories of altered cats and females are usually smaller than unneutered toms but are more fiercely defended, particularly if the cat has kittens. Cats that share territorial boundaries avoid conflict by establishing "freeways" through the home ranges, often fences or walls.

during mating; at other times they tend to seek the companionship of their own gender. An exception to this is the mother-son bond—male cats will usually continue to have a relationship with their mothers as long as they are not separated for any length of time.

Female cats have a social hierarchy as well, but it's arranged more loosely. With each new litter, a queen increases her social status. A queen with kittens, regardless of prior social status, dramatically moves up the social ladder. Female cats cooperate with each other more than male cats, and sometimes nurse and take care of each other's kittens while the other female takes a break or hunts. Sometimes, however, male cats will band together to defend a common area from intruders.

While females hold less territory than the males, they defend it more fiercely, particularly if they have kittens to protect. A mother cat is usually less tolerant of intruders than a dominant male. When defending her kittens, a mother cat usually does not bother with the ritual posturing common among cats, but immediately attacks viciously not only other cats, but dogs, foxes, humans (sometimes), and any other creature that threatens her litter.

When neutered or spayed, male and female cats quickly lose their place in the feline hierarchy, and cats that are altered before establishing their rank have no status in the social order. However, this is not a good excuse for failing to spay or neuter your cats. Altered cats are still territorial, and will still have their home bases and home ranges. Their area tends to be smaller but, like the females, they tend to defend it more fiercely. Domestic cats tend to be more tolerant than wild or feral cats.

Fighting

While cats will fight if necessary, they will generally avoid down-and-dirty fighting when they can, and will rely instead on vocal and postural threats to challenge foes and appeasement rituals to back down from stronger opponents. A common way to resolve conflict is a staring match (see page 61). These safety mechanisms are typical among predatory species that can inflict a great deal of damage with the survival weapons Mother Nature has given them. To protect themselves, most predators develop a strict social order that allows them to get along with each other. The dominance hierarchy is one of those safety mechanisms. Not only is it dangerous to fight, it is also time- and energy-consuming. Cats just don't have the leisure to attack every foe, particularly in high-population-density areas where they are likely to meet many of their own kind on any given day. Therefore, cats are strongly motivated to deflect actual fighting, and as social animals they have developed ways of avoiding aggression. When they do resort to fighting, the fights are usually savage but short, with the loser escaping as soon as possible.

Clubbing

A little-understood feline social behavior is called clubbing. Both male and female cats gather at an apparently appointed meeting ground, usually in neutral territory, and peacefully sit near one another, groom, and socialize. After a few hours of this amiable mingling, the cats go back home to their own territories. Occasionally mating takes place at these gatherings, but this apparently is not the main purpose of them. Biologists don't understand this behavior, but it obviously fulfills some important social need. Perhaps this behavior is another way of defusing violence in the cat community; by getting to know one another in neutral territory, the need to fight when they next meet may be minimized.

Indoor Cats

Indoor cats do not lose their territorial instinct, but the territorial boundaries in multicat homes are usually small and can vary depending upon the time of day. Members of an indoor-only clan usually arrange themselves into a more or less amiable hierarchy, with one dominant cat in charge and all the rest of the cats sharing middle rank. Favorite sleeping spots, furniture, the rug by the fire, or even a sunny spot by the window can be claimed by the dominant cat. The other cats work out their territory, laying claim to a particular area they can feel is theirs alone. However, these areas may change depending on the time of day. Many indoor cats have "time-share" arrangements for favored spots; this behavior is thought to be a version of the time-sharing territorial behavior cats exhibit in the wild, and is very common in multicat households.

For example, Punkin, my Abyssinian, lays no claim to the surface of my bed until my bedtime; then the bed is all hers and she'll attack any feline intruders. But during the day, the bed belongs to Clancy and Goose, my two males. If Punkin tries to climb aboard before their shift is over, they run her off.

Domestic cats are not above using subterfuge and trickery to get favored sleeping spots. Pooka, our Siamese look-alike, is downright tricky when she wants a sleeping spot occupied by another cat. First, she'll walk up and stand over the sleeper, much too close, invading her victim's personal space and making her nervous (she never tries this with the boys). Often, her victim will give in and move away and then Pooka will happily take over the now prewarmed spot, but since Pooka is not the top cat in the household, that doesn't always work. Occasionally, she resorts to trickery and makes a great show of finding something interesting within her victim's line of sight. It might be a scrap of paper, a toy, or sometimes nothing at all. With our smarter cats, this doesn't always work, but with Punkin it works every time. She'll get up to see what is so interesting, and

Pooka will zip into her sleeping spot with a smug look on her face. Punkin never learns.

Over time, the territorial boundaries may blur until the cats share the entire household domain more or less peacefully, defending it from all outside intruders. All cats need at least one spot to call their own, however, and overcrowding is as upsetting to cats as it is to humans.

Sometimes, particularly if overcrowded, one or two lower-ranking felines become scapegoats for the group and are universally abused by the community. Biologists believe this to be a social safety valve that prevents the feline social structure from breaking down into chaos. This analysis gives us an interesting glimpse into certain human behaviors as well.

A single indoor-only cat, alone all day and deprived of feline company, can suffer from loneliness and may become depressed, as we do when we are kept from the company of our family and friends. While cats get many of their social needs from their human companions, it is wise to provide your indoor cat with a feline companion.

Sexual Behavior

For cats, as for all creatures that reproduce sexually, the key to survival is reproduction, and that's why much of feline behavior and social structure is associated with procreation. For example, the tom's habit of spraying to mark his territory is sexual in origin. The behavior is dependent on the presence of male sex hormones, which is why neutering usually ends spraying. Sex hormones motivate both male and female cats from the moment they reach puberty and their reproductive cycles begin.

A breeding female feline is called a queen. A queen usually goes into her first heat between eight months and one year, although some purebreds are slower to mature.

A queen normally experiences several heat cycles, called *estrus,* in late winter to early spring, and late spring to early summer, but the queen's seasonal cycles can begin as early as January and can end as late as October in the Northern Hemisphere. In the Southern Hemisphere, the heat cycles are exactly the opposite. Cats ordinarily do not go into heat from October through December.

The day's length regulates the cat's heat cycles. The onset of ovarian follicle growth is caused by increased light stimulation on the hypothalamus. More simply, when the days get longer, the brain tells the body it's time to mate. A day length of 12 to 14 hours seems optimal for bringing queens into heat. Exceptions exist, however. Indoor-only cats, affected by the indoor artificial light, can go into heat any time of year.

Estrus usually lasts for 5 to 8 days, but can be as long as 20. The heat cycle consists of three stages:
1. *Proestrus* is the period before estrus. It typically lasts only a day or so. In proestrus, the queen may become more loving to you and to the other humans and animals in the household. She may want to be petted more often, to sit in your lap, or to be near you. It's also possible you won't notice any change in her behavior during this period.
2. The second stage is *estrus* proper, when the queen is sexually receptive. When estrus begins, it's usually obvious. The queen meows incessantly; this distinctive sound is known as *calling.* She rolls on the ground and rubs up against you and the furniture. She may pace back and forth and seem agitated and restless. She may also assume the mating position called *lordosis.* She crouches low with her back swayed and her tail held to one side. She treads with her rear feet while calling repeatedly. If allowed outside, the queen may disappear for several days, and come home tired, hungry, and most likely pregnant.
3. *Interestrus* is the third stage, the period of ovarian and sexual inactivity following estrus. It normally lasts from a number of days to three or four weeks.

Queens can go into heat several times during the yearly cycles if copulation and impregnation do not occur. Having your normally calm and quiet cat prowling around yowling at the top of her lungs is distracting at best. Spay Fluffy if you don't intend to breed her. Spaying ends the annoying behavior associated with estrus and is kinder to your cat; it's cruel to allow her to suffer repeated sexual frustration.

Unneutered adult males (toms) also go through a period of *rut* that peaks in springtime and declines in fall. It's not clear whether the photocycle governs the tom's sexual cycles like the queen's, or if the tom's rut is triggered by the availability of sexually receptive females and the pheromones queens in heat produce.

In general, male cats reach puberty and begin producing *androgen,* or sex hormones, at around nine months. From then on, they spend most of their time seeking receptive females and defending their territory from other males.

When a queen goes into estrus, she produces high levels of pheromones with which to attract her mate. Calling also serves as a "come-and-get-it" signal to the male. Toms can perceive these olfactory and auditory signals from far away. This is why neighborhood toms line up on the doorstep when your queen is in heat. The tom shows his sexual readiness by pacing back and forth, spraying urine, licking his penis, and yowling.

Fights for the opportunity to mate may erupt between the competing toms, but female cats have minds of their own and do not necessarily mate with the fight's winner. Seemingly unimpressed by the macho displays, they sometimes mate with losing males far down on the hierarchy ladder. Queens often mate with more than one male during any given estrus period as well. It's possible for kittens in the same litter to have different fathers.

Tomcats are usually not particular about the breed, age, health, appearance, or familial relationship of a mating partner. Toms will readily mate with their grandmothers, mothers, sisters, and daughters. In humans that's called incest; in felines, it's called inbreeding. Familial relationship means nothing to queens, either,

but queens are, in general, more selective about their mating partners. This is true of many animals; the female has more invested in one mating than does the male.

Mating

Before the actual mating occurs, a ritual courting takes place in which the tom cautiously approaches and calls to the object of his affections. At first, the queen may snarl and strike out at the male. The tom accepts this without taking offense and waits some distance away, watching the female for signs of readiness. The male may make plaintive yowls called *singing* as if to reassure the female of his good intentions. An inexperienced tom may try to hurry the female and earn himself swipes from the female's ready claws. Rape doesn't exist in feline society; one doesn't rape a female that has five daggers on each paw and is not afraid of using them. Mating is the female's choice.

When the female is ready, she gives an *appeasement cry* to show she is receptive. She assumes the mating position with her tail to one side to allow the tom to penetrate. The tom approaches from behind and mounts the queen, grasping the back of her neck in his teeth. He places his forelegs over her shoulders and straddles her pelvic area. When the position is correct, the tom inserts his penis into the queen's vagina. Actual genital contact lasts only a few seconds; ejaculation is almost immediate.

When the tom ejaculates, the queen lets out a high-pitched scream and turns on the male, seemingly enraged. She may strike at him, hiss, or snarl. This sudden mood swing is unique among domestic animals, and is probably due to the spiny barbs covering the male's penis. The barbs violently stimulate the female's vagina, and this stimulation triggers a chain of hormonal reactions, producing ovulation.

Felines are *induced ovulators,* which means copulation must take place for ovulation to occur. Ovulation ordinarily takes place 24 to 30 hours after copulation. Provoking this hormonal response may be the sole purpose of the penis's barbs, or they may also help the male maintain penetration. No one really knows for sure. Regardless, they're probably responsible for the yowl and the aggressive reaction of the female following mating.

Following copulation, the queen rolls on the ground and licks her genitals. The tom withdraws a short distance away to lick his penis and paws. After an intermission of several minutes to several hours, the mating ritual begins again. Cats can couple many times within the estrus period, and the queen may mate with more than one tom during her heat period.

Maternal Behavior

You may have heard of Scarlett, the brave calico cat in Port Washing-

Persian mother with her three-week-old kitten. Cats are dedicated and protective mothers.

ton, New York, who on March 29, 1996 walked through fire to rescue her five kittens from a burning building. One by one, she carried them to safety through the fiery blaze, at nearly the cost of her own life. When the firefighters arrived, her eyes were blistered shut and she was so badly burned she could barely walk, but, nevertheless, she tenderly nuzzled each kitten and used her sense of smell to make sure all were safe. The story galvanized the nation's animal lovers, and donations and offers of homes for Scarlett and her kittens came in from all across the country.

Scarlett's story is an extreme example of the strong bond that exists between a mother cat and her kittens. Blind and deaf at birth, kittens are virtually helpless for their first few weeks of life. Without their mother's dedicated care, they would not survive. Mother Nature, in her wisdom, gave female cats strong maternal instincts for the preservation of the species. The maternal instinct is so strong that mother cats will often willingly nurse kittens that are not theirs. Some mother cats will even foster the young of other species. A friend of mine saved a baby raccoon that way; the mother cat took to him just fine and seemed to consider him one of her own. The raccoon grew up believing he was a cat.

Instinct is not the only source of maternal behavior, of course; early learning plays a role in the development of good mothering skills. Mothers also gain knowledge from practice; an experienced queen is more likely to provide good care for her kittens since she learns from her previous mistakes. Cats weaned too early may have difficulty when it comes their turn to raise their litters.

Male cats take no part in kitten rearing; their involvement in the production of kittens generally ends with the completion of the sex act. Most tomcats pay little attention to kittens—theirs or anybody else's—and may even try to kill them. Male lions exhibit the same behavior; they kill the cubs of other males to make the females go back into heat more quickly, thereby insuring the new male's genetic survival.

Female cats, however, are dedicated, protective mothers that care for their kittens, teach them all the skills they need to know to survive in adulthood, and fiercely defend them when they are threatened. Since, in the wild, a cat's kin do not gather around to help the mother care for her charges, it's up to her to insure her kittens' survival.

The Kittens' Early Life

For the first three weeks of life, when the kittens are most vulnerable and reliant on Mom's care, the mother spends most of her time with her kittens, taking only short breaks to get food and water and to relieve herself. She spends an estimated 70 percent of her time nursing during this stage. She washes each kitten regularly, licking her *perineum* (the area under the tail) to stimulate urination and defecation, since kittens cannot relieve themselves on their own for the first several weeks of life. She circles them with her body to encourage them to suckle, and uses her strong sense of smell to tell them apart and to make sure all are accounted for. Even when she is away from the nest, she is constantly aware of the kittens and will come running at any cries of distress.

The kittens usually choose a particular nipple, locating it most likely by scent, but possibly by location as well. During nursing, the kittens first exhibit the kneading action with their paws, a behavior many cats continue into adulthood. The kittens form a strong bond with their mother almost immediately upon birth. This bond is vital to the kittens' normal development.

The kittens' eyes open between the seventh and tenth day, although a rare kitten will be precocious or a late bloomer. The kittens' eyesight remains poor for several more weeks. Born with their ear canals closed, newborn kittens' hearing is poor for the first few weeks as well; therefore, the sense of smell is vital during early development. A kitten may totter out of the nest at this stage, or be dragged out while attached to Mom. Out of the nest, the kitten will make an intense repeated cry that is sometimes outside the range of human hearing until the mother responds with a particular call of her own and carries the stray back to her proper place. She does this by gripping the scruff of the neck; when this is done by Mom it generally does not hurt the kitten, but *you* should never pick up a kitten or cat that way. Leave scruff carrying to the experts. Researchers believe that mother cats can distinguish between their kittens by their individual cries.

If the mother decides that the nest is no longer a safe or convenient place for her kittens, she will move them, one by one, to a new location. A nervous mother may move her kittens numerous times, but generally the mother relocates her litter only if their safety is in question or if the nest becomes too small or unclean. The mother may also move the litter to be closer to a source of food, particularly when the kittens begin to eat on their own.

After three weeks, the mother leaves the nest for longer periods, and becomes more reluctant to provide around-the-clock nursing services. This is due to the pain of the kittens' sharp milk teeth, the burden of providing all nourishment to rapidly growing offspring, and the kittens' changed behavior. Their growth and behavioral changes alter Mom's response to them.

Weaning

The kittens now have to initiate nursing themselves when they become hungry; the mother no longer encourages the behavior, and although the kittens would be happy to continue nursing forever, Mom has begun the weaning process. As time goes on, she will move away when the kittens try to nurse, or even cuff them if they harass her too much. This encourages them to move on to solid food. While she will still spend much of her time with her kittens, she will sit beside them or watch them from a perch that they cannot reach. They must learn independence.

When they become so large that she cannot provide adequate nutrition to her brood and herself, she begins to provide another food source for her kittens—solid food. In the wild, that means bringing meat and other food home for the kittens starting at about two weeks of age. In domestication, that means bringing tidbits or encouraging the kittens to feed from the feeding dishes. Unlike female dogs, mother cats do not regurgitate food for their offspring. In domestication, solid food should be offered at four to five weeks. By the time the kittens are 8 weeks old, they are fully weaned, but may continue to try to nurse until 12 weeks.

Teaching the Kittens to Survive

After her "milk bar" position is over, a mother cat still has work to do to help her kittens survive in adulthood. She does this by teaching the kittens important lessons like hunting, and covering their feces and urine. Quite a number of studies have been done on the effect of Mom's teaching. They show that kittens can learn difficult or complex tasks when first taught by their mother, while, without help, the kittens are unable to perform the task or do it poorly. Cats learn just as much by observation as they do by trial and error. Litter box training is a snap when the mother cat is around—if you present the litter box, the mother will teach her charges how to use it through her example, another reason kittens need time with their mothers.

Mother cats will also teach their offspring how to hunt. If allowed outdoors, Mom will bring live prey home to the kittens when they are about six to eight weeks old so they can practice their pouncing and "killing bite" techniques. Kittens taught by their mothers become far better hunters than those that miss this early schooling.

Kittens that are separated from their mothers for a period of months may not be warmly welcomed if returned to their mother. Mom may not recognize the kittens as her own offspring and may even attack them. Only if the kittens are left with their mother indefinitely will the maternal bond remain strong. The mother cat will continue to exhibit maternal behavior toward her kittens even after they are fully mature.

Sleep and Dreaming

In the words of American writer Joseph Wood Krutch, "Cats are rather delicate creatures and they are subject to a good many ailments, but I never heard of one who suffered from insomnia." Cats are well known for their impressive ability to sleep despite all kinds of commotion. Because cats are such enthusiastic sleepers, they have been the subjects of many sleep studies. In fact, much of what we know about sleep comes from the study of cats.

Experts are still not entirely sure why animals—or humans, for that matter—need to sleep. Some think that sleep is necessary to refresh our supply of neurotransmitters, the chemicals responsible for transmitting nerve impulses. Others believe that during sleep the brain organizes and processes memories of happenings from earlier in the day. Still others speculate that sleep refreshes the body and mind and allows them to recuperate from the activities of the waking hours, recharging the cat's (and our) batteries, so to speak. Some theorize that sleep is a way to conserve energy among animals that maintain a constant body temperature; cats use less energy when asleep. These theories all seem credible, but no one really knows for sure. That sleep serves a vital physiological function is clear, however. Without sleep, judgment is impaired, vocalization becomes difficult, reflexes slow, vision blurs, and the subject becomes irritable and confused. Lack of sleep can even kill.

On average, cats sleep up to two thirds of each day or up to 16 hours out of every 24. Humans average about 7.5 hours of sleep per day. While humans generally sleep for a certain number of hours a night, cats do not get all their sleep in one long stretch. Cats spread out their sleep into shorter segments, which is why the term "catnap" was coined.

Two distinct phases of sleep exist—slow-wave or "quiet" sleep and rapid eye movement (REM) or "active" sleep. Of those 16 hours of sleep, 9 to 12 are spent in slow-wave sleep (SWS). In SWS, also called "sleep of the mind," the cat's rapid-fire brain activity slows and acquires a more rhythmical pattern. The brain wave activity during this kind of sleep recorded on an electroencephalograph (EEG) shows high-voltage,

An Abyssinian cat. Cats spend a good portion of their lives sleeping.

slow-wave patterns, thus the name. Fluffy relaxes, but not so much that she can't hold up her head. In SWS she typically rests in the *sternally recumbent* or sphinx position—head up, feet out in front or tucked underneath. Breathing is slow and deep, and the cat's nictitating membranes (her inner eyelids) are drawn over the eyes. A cat can be easily awakened from slow-wave sleep. This type of sleep rests the mind.

Four to seven of a cat's sleeping hours are spent in REM sleep, during which the sleeper's eyes dart rapidly back and forth beneath the closed eyelids and nictitating membranes and the body's muscles relax completely and become flaccid. This is when you will see Fluffy curled into a ball or sacked out on her side. REM sleep rests the body, and is also called *paradoxical sleep* because, although the body is deeply asleep, the cat's mind is highly active; the electrical impulses present during REM sleep rival that of waking brain patterns. An EEG scan shows the brain waves to be low-voltage and fast-wave. This stage of sleep is very deep. While you can awaken a cat from SWS merely by quietly walking into the room, much more stimulation is needed to rouse a cat from REM sleep. Cats suddenly awakened from REM sleep behave very much as humans do when suddenly roused from REM sleep—they appear startled, disoriented, and groggy. It takes them a moment to wake up and realize where they are.

Fluffy alternates between the two sleep types. She begins her sleep period in slow-wave sleep; 10 to 30 minutes after falling asleep, she will move into REM sleep for 6 or 7 minutes. She will then lapse back into SWS for 20 to 30 minutes. Between sleep periods, she may wake, stretch, scratch her post, catch a quick bite, move to a more comfortable spot, and then enter the next sleep cycle.

Observing where Fluffy sleeps can tell you quite a bit about her personality and habits. A cat that is confident and comfortable around her human companions sleeps where she chooses—the middle of the floor, for example, or beside you on the couch. A more cautious cat will seek a safe place to sleep, one elevated to give her a better vantage point, or sheltered to give protection from possible attackers.

Do Cats Dream?

Unfortunately, no cat has kindly shared this information with us; however, experts have determined by EEG scans that cats in REM sleep produce essentially the same electrical brain impulses that humans do in REM sleep. Since humans dream during REM sleep, it's conceivable that cats dream as well. Cats in REM sleep twitch, jump, and jerk, and some appear to be running in their sleep. Ears twitch, whiskers quiver, tongues flick, tails twitch, and jaws snap during these episodes. Cats also mutter, meow, and growl, rather like humans who mumble and talk in their sleep. Cats also have been known to snore.

The evidence does lead us to conclude that cats dream, but we can't really know with certainty; nor can we rule it out. The more interesting question might be, if cats dream, what do they dream about? Do they dream of mountains of imaginary kitty treats? Do they chase make-believe mice? Run away from dream dogs? Battle imagined rivals? We'll never know, but we can speculate that cats dream about the things that they experience during their waking hours, as we do.

Biorhythms

The other eight hours or so of Fluffy's day are spent awake playing, hunting, eating, using her litter box, grooming, socializing, and the ever popular staring contentedly into space. The biological rhythms that determine the pattern of sleep and wakefulness are known as *circadian rhythms*. This biological clock is approximately tied to the 24-hour day we enjoy on this planet. Since cats are predators, in the wild they generally follow the activity schedules of their prey: small rodents. That's why cats are *crepuscular*—most active at dawn and dusk—because mice and rats forage for food during these hours when fewer of their natural enemies are around. Millions of years of adaptation have turned the cat into a nocturnal animal, like her prey. This is why training sessions with your cat are best done when you come home from work or early in the morning before you leave. Fluffy is more active and alert at those times.

Predators such as cats tend to sleep more than their prey. It's supposed that they do this to conserve energy for the next period of hunting, when a great deal of energy is expended; therefore, they tend to catch naps when they can and hunt when the opportunity presents itself. Prey animals, on the other hand, sleep much less than predators. For one thing, they must consume more plant matter to support their body weight than a predator must consume of its protein-dense prey. For another, being prey animals, they must be vigilant against danger.

Cats are good at adapting to their environment, so their sleep habits vary depending upon the environment. A domestic cat kept indoors and subjected to artificial lights and her human's regular sleeping habits and predicable schedule will adapt to her owner's schedule, to an extent. You may still find your cat companion pouncing on your toes in the middle of the night or be awakened by a frolicking feline at dawn.

Grooming

Fastidious grooming is one of the things that makes cats such good companions. They keep themselves clean and neat with little help from us. Cats are naturally clean animals and generally devote between 8 and 15 percent of their waking hours to grooming, which would be like one of us spending more than two hours scrubbing in the shower every day. Some cat breeds, like the longhaired Persian, need more help from their humans to keep their hair free of mats, but shorthaired cats usually need little assistance. Unlike dogs, cats generally do not need regular bathing to keep looking and smelling good.

Grooming appears to be instinctual behavior, and kittens as young as three weeks old can be seen making their first grooming attempts. By six weeks kittens are usually adept. Cats expend quite a lot of water to produce their cleansing saliva—a cat may lose as much moisture through saliva as through urination. Since the cat's ancestor is the African wildcat, a desert animal that can little afford to waste water unnecessarily, grooming must serve an important function indeed to be worth the

Cats groom more in warm weather than in cold because the evaporation of saliva helps keep the cat cool.

proof the coat and provides the cat with vitamin D. Also, grooming is vital to parasite control; a well-groomed cat will have fewer fleas, ticks, and other parasites than a cat that grooms less frequently. In addition, clean skin is healthy skin, and cats have a much lower incidence of bacterial skin infections than do dogs. Experts theorize that either the grooming itself removes harmful bacteria, or some element in the cat's saliva reduces the growth of bacteria.

But the most important reason of all for grooming is that it removes dirt, food, and odors from the cat's fur. Since cats are predators, they naturally end up well perfumed by their prey after a meal. If they didn't clean up after eating, the odors of their prey would remain on their fur and it would be very hard to sneak up on their next mobile meal without being detected. Also, the scent could attract the attention of larger, fiercer predators that Fluffy wisely would like to avoid. Cats' sensitivity to these odors makes them fastidious about their grooming.

The cat's tongue is covered with hooked, backward-pointing scales called *papillae*. These scales make the tongue good for combing the fur and skin. Fluffy also uses the front paws to wash areas inaccessible to the tongue, such as the head, face, neck, and ears. On occasion, cats also use their teeth and claws to remove particularly stubborn debris or parasites. They usually follow a set grooming pattern, generally beginning with the head, moving to

water. And it does. Cats groom for a number of very good reasons. For one thing, grooming helps Fluffy regulate her temperature. Since cats have few *atrichial sweat glands,* the kind that secrete watery sweat to help dissipate heat, the evaporation of saliva on the coat substitutes for sweat to help keep them cool in hot weather, a boon for a desert animal. Grooming keeps the fur neat and free of loose hair and snarls, and this helps cats regulate body temperature as well. A clear, well-maintained coat has cushions of air between the hairs, which act as insulation from the cold. Grooming also spreads sebum, a fatty secretion from glands in the skin, onto the fur, which helps water-the back and sides, and finishing with the hind end. During really thorough grooming sessions, cats will also clean their feet, tail, belly, and genital region. Some experts believe that grooming, like sleeping, is governed by the feline biological clock.

Like humans, some cats take a great deal of pride in their appearance, while others are haphazard in their grooming efforts. It's a good idea to watch Fluffy and learn her patterns because sudden changes in grooming habits, either increases or decreases, can signal emotional or physical distress. This will be covered in more detail in Chapter 8.

Most cat owners have noticed a grooming phenomenon called *displacement activity,* in which Fluffy has a spat with her housemate, or misjudges a leap to the counter and then grooms herself to recover from her embarrassment, fear, or annoyance. Cats will also groom when they are undecided about the best course of action in a particular situation. Call to your cat—does she ever pause to give herself a few licks while deciding whether walking over to see what you want is worth the effort? This displacement activity is a way of coping with conflict; in essence, it gives Fluffy something comforting to do while she sorts it all out.

Allogrooming

Cats usually groom themselves, but on occasion they do groom each other. This is called *allogrooming,* and it is most commonly seen between mother cats and their kit-

tens, cats that have grown up together, and siblings. Mother cats groom their kittens from the moment they are born. Kittens must receive grooming from their mother to develop normally and also to survive the first three weeks of life when mother cats lick the kittens' genitals to stimulate urination and defecation. Without this stimulation the kittens would die. By six weeks, the kittens are grooming themselves and their mother. This mutual grooming seems pleasurable for all and is part of the close bond kittens and mother share.

However, unrelated adult cats can also indulge in mutual grooming if they feel a strong bond to another cat. For example, when Clancy came to live with us, Goose, our older neutered male, took Clancy under his wing, so to speak, and often groomed the younger cat, which they both seemed to enjoy. I have no idea if that had anything to do with Clancy's obvious lack of mothering, but it's possible, I suppose, that Goose sensed Clancy's need and responded to it.

This type of bond is a kind of displaced parenting behavior in which the older cat feels the need to nurture the younger. More common in females, this type of bond does occur in both genders. It can occur across species, too; cats that are strongly bonded to their humans will often give their favorite person a bath. So if Fluffy likes to lick you, consider it a compliment. Grooming your cat is also an excellent way to cement the emotional bond between you.

Aging

As cats age, their bodies go through changes. In general, cats are considered in the *geriatric* life stage when they reach ten years of age. At first, the signs of aging are not obvious. Perhaps the cat begins to sleep more, becomes less playful, exhibits behavioral changes, and gains or loses weight. As a cat ages, she becomes less active and more susceptible to certain diseases and illnesses. Her metabolic rate may decrease. She becomes less agile, less flexible, and her eyesight and hearing may become less acute. For this reason, the cat's litter box, food dishes, and bedding should be put in easily accessible places.

Old cats are also more susceptible to heat and cold. Keep the house at a consistent, comfortable temperature. The cat may spend less time grooming. Obese cats or cats who have arthritis have difficulty grooming themselves, and so put off the duty that they attended to so religiously during their youth. These changes are a normal part of aging.

Be alert for symptoms that may occur as your cat ages: excessive drinking and frequent urination (possible signs of diabetes or kidney problems); lumps under the skin (tumors); hyperactivity, wakefulness, thirst, diarrhea, increased appetite accompanied by weight loss (hyperthyroidism); bad breath, drooling, pain when eating (tooth decay, gingivitis); stiff or painful movement (arthritis); weight loss (liver or kidney failure); lack of appetite, frequent vomiting, and diarrhea that may contain blood (pancreatitis); difficulty breathing, coughing, shortness of breath, abdominal distention, weight gain, and reduced tolerance to exercise (heart disease).

Cats become set in their ways, and your cat may be easily irritated and less tolerant of environmental changes. For this reason, avoid introducing new pets, or subjecting your senior feline to rough handling and loud noises.

The senior cat may forget her litter box training because of increased urination or bladder or gastrointestinal problems. When your cat begins to show signs of aging, it is a good time to reinforce toilet training.

Cat Years	Human Years
6 months	10 years
8 months	13 years
12 months	15 years
2 years	24 years
4 years	32 years
6 years	40 years
8 years	48 years
10 years	56 years
12 years	64 years
14 years	72 years
16 years	80 years
18 years	88 years
20 years	96 years
21 years	100 years

(Courtesy of StarKist Foods)

Chapter Five

Learning Your Cat's Cues

Anyone who claims that a cat cannot give a dirty look either has never kept a cat or is singularly unobservant.

—Maurice Burton

Cats let us know their feelings clearly if we know how to read their signals. Based on their reactions to situations, we can conclude that cats have the same basic emotions we do. When challenged by a rival, a cat feels anger. When threatened by a stronger opponent or faced with an unknown threat, a cat knows fear. Cats willingly demonstrate feelings of affection, both for other cats and for humans. It's well known to veterinarians that cats experience both anxiety and depression. Cats use a variety of vocal, physical, and olfactory signals to communicate their feelings and needs. Learning to recognize Tiger's emotional state requires nothing more than learning his cues—his body language. Since a cat can be quite subtle in his messages, an understanding of these cues is vital to understanding your cat. Learning his normal behavior is also important because you will be able to recognize changes that may indicate illness or distress.

Vocal Language

Wild and feral cats—cats that have little or no contact with humans—do not vocalize the way domestic cats do. Many experts believe domestic cats learn to vocalize differently from wild or feral cats. When your cat looks up and meows at you to get attention, he is exhibiting learned behavior. Cats are very adaptable, and learn this kind of vocalization as part of the emotional bond they develop with humans.

Spook, a battered feral tom that has since passed onto the Rainbow Bridge, showed up in my backyard one October. Completely wild and obviously never a house cat, Spook never learned to trust me enough to allow me to touch him, even after a year of regular feeding. However, we learned to communicate after a fashion and we did establish a

Cats use a variety of vocal and postural signals to get their wishes across to their human owners.

relationship, a bit one-sided, to be sure. He came and sat outside the kitchen door, waiting for me to notice and feed him. When I stepped outside with his food, he'd run a dozen steps away and watch me warily from behind the bushes, ears flattened and eyes dilated, until I'd gone back inside. Then he'd approach, eat the food, and go about the important business of refreshing his territorial markers in my yard. Sometimes I'd creep down the steps until we were about 5 feet (1.5 m) apart and talk softly to him. Spook would gaze back with eyes full of suspicion and mistrust. He came for the handouts but he never trusted my motives.

In the year I fed Spook, I never heard him utter any sound other than a hiss. Unlike our indoor-only cats, he didn't meow when he was hungry. He simply sat outside the door and waited in silence.

This is the way with wild and feral felines; they do not vocalize as domestic cats do. They know meows may frighten away their potential dinner or invite the unwanted attention of larger predators, so they learn silence as a way of survival. The only exceptions to this are the vocal sounds made during fighting, mating, and kitten rearing. Adult feral cats have no use for please-feed-me meows and do not learn them. They rely instead almost entirely on olfactory communication (see page 63) and body language when communicating with other cats.

Domestic cats, however, learn to vocalize to a much greater extent from their close association with humans. Cats, supreme watchers that they are, see that we communicate by sound, and they vocalize when they want our attention. Also, cat owners are well known for talking to their cats, and cats learn from this. They quickly learn that vocal communication is rewarded by their human companions: A plaintive meow produces a can of cat food or a treat; a yowl is rewarded with a session of petting or play, or an opened door. All of the sounds a cat learns to use to communicate with humans are in their biological repertoire—they just learn to use them to a greater extent and in different ways than they would in the wild.

A cat's repertoire of sounds depends a great deal on learned behavior. A cat whose owner talks to him and pays attention to his answers is more likely to develop vocal communication skills. A house cat that is ignored by his human family and cursed when he opens his mouth will not develop the same communication skills because he is not rewarded for that behavior.

It also depends to a certain extent on genetics. Kittens know instinctively how to hiss at frightening objects, purr when content, and make distinctive calls to their mothers when in distress. Female cats in heat belt out a particularly annoying bellow when calling for a mate. Some cat breeds, for example, the Siamese and other Oriental breeds, seem genetically prone to vocalizing their feelings more than other breeds. In fact, Siamese are known for incessant childlike meows for reasons not obvious to their nonplussed human owners. Perhaps, like some people, they just like hearing themselves talk. Other breeds, such as the Abyssinian and the Persian, are known for vocalizing less than other breeds and, when they do vocalize, their voices tend to be soft and unobtrusive. Since these two breeds are on the opposite ends of the cat spectrum in activity level, the tendency to vocalize doesn't seem to be tied to that trait.

At any rate, cats use a variety of meows, murmurs, yowls, and screams to communicate with other cats and with humans. You can interpret these as greetings, demands, pleas, complaints, or challenges, depending on the tone. As you get

Some breeds are more vocal than others. Oriental breeds like the Siamese and the Oriental Shorthair are particularly known for their vocal talents.

better acquainted with your feline friend, you'll become familiar with his individual vocabulary and know when he wants to eat, play, be petted, or just be left alone to sleep in the sun.

Although people generally use the word "meow" to imitate the sound their cats make, cats actually have a wide range of vocalizations for a variety of situations. Dr. Mildred Moelk is credited with much of what we know about cat chat. Over a five-year period in the late 1930s and early 1940s, Dr. Moelk studied feline vocalization. She determined that cats make 16 distinct vocal patterns broken into three sound-pattern groups: murmur patterns, vowel patterns, and strained intensity patterns. According to Dr. Moelk's research, feline sounds do not translate to words but to the cat's emotional state, and cat lovers can use the sounds to understand the cat's state of mind.

Sound Patterns

Murmurs are made with the mouth closed and are used to indicate contentment or friendliness. These sounds include purring, greetings or requests, calls, and acknowledgments.

The vowel patterns include the more typical meow sounds and are made by opening and then gradually closing the mouth. These sounds indicate demands, begging, bewilderment sounds, complaints, mild mating cries, and anger wails.

Strained intensity patterns are made by holding the mouth open and tense, and forcing breath through the mouth. These sounds indicate that the cat is in a highly emotional state and include growls, snarls, intense mating cries, pain cries, and spitting.

Purring

Purring is probably the second most recognized feline sound. Kittens begin purring about two days after birth. The queen also purrs when the kittens are nursing, possibly to reassure and comfort them or because she enjoys the nursing process and the connection to her kittens. Kittens can feel as well as hear their mother's purring, so purring may also act as a dinner bell.

As adults, cats purr when they are contented, are pleased to see their human or cat friends, and are hungry. Female cats purr when they are courting and mating.

Cats also purr when they are in distress. The *distress purr* occurs when a cat is in a stressful situation and needs comforting. Goose, a somewhat anxious cat to begin with, purrs up a storm when I take him to the veterinarian, and he certainly isn't displaying his contentment. Cats have been known to purr when ill, in labor, frightened, or even dying. Cat behaviorists now believe cats can purr in response to any strong emotion. It appears cats can purr at will; it's not an involuntary response to emotion.

No one really knows how cats purr. They purr while both inhaling and exhaling, and can purr for long periods without apparent fatigue. One former theory, now generally discounted by researchers, is that turbulence in the bloodstream causes purring. Many researchers today believe purring is caused by unsynchronized movements of the muscles of the diaphragm and the larynx. Purring is produced by air resonating in the larynx, partly controlled by the vocal cords' movements.

Not everyone agrees with this theory, however. At least one expert believes purring is caused by the fluttering motion of the cat's excessively long soft palate. The feline soft palate contains muscle fibers a cat can control, making it possible for controlled motion of the soft palate to cause purring.

However they do it, cats are pleasant company when they make their soothing purrs. As with all cat characteristics, purring styles and pitches exist; some cats have dainty, almost inaudible, purrs while others have purrs that can be heard across the room. Some cats purr at the drop of a hat; others reserve purring for special occasions only. If your cat doesn't purr, it's not cause for concern since it seems to serve an emotional rather than a physical need.

Growling

All cats, wild and domestic, growl as an aggressive or defensive warning. Although cats occasionally growl playfully, as dogs do, the body language accompanying the growl indicates whether the cat is truly angry. The sound can range from a low grumble to an open-mouthed yowling growl that shows that the cat feels threatened and is ready to take offense. Growling can progress to full-scale screams of rage or fear if the threatening encroacher doesn't retreat.

Hissing and Spitting

When threatened, irritated, or angry, cats expel air sharply through their mouths in a distinctive sound called hissing. Spitting is similar to hissing, but it has a sharper and more explosive sound. Although cats sometimes hiss playfully, they usually make these sounds when they become angry. It means, *"Leave me alone!"* or *"Back off!"*

Hissing serves as a vocal warning. It means that the cat is angry or defensive.

Chattering

Another distinctive feline sound is chattering. When Tiger sees a fly, bird, moth, or other winged creature outside the window, he will sometimes make a staccato, stuttering type of meow. Researchers are not sure why. Since cats seem to have an instinctive aversion to flies and other flying insects, the sound may serve as a warning. Or it might be simply a sound of frustration because the prey is out of reach. Toms waiting for queens to become ready to receive their affections will also chatter. It could be that chattering expresses or releases emotional tension.

Body Language

Cats use body postures to communicate their intentions and emotions. Adult cats in the wild rely almost exclusively on body language and scent-marking to communicate to others of their species. By watching Tiger's body language, you can gauge his feelings quite well. A cat's face is especially significant in assessing his mood, and certain ear and head postures often precede body stance when showing emotion.

A cat uses a variety of body postures to show his affection for humans and for other animals. A friendly, confident cat walks with his tail held high. The tip of the tail sometimes curves slightly to form a furry question mark shape. His ears are upright and perky, his pupils are normal size, neither constricted nor dilated, and his whiskers are spread and relaxed. A cat approaching you in this manner shows he's happy to see you. Other clear signs of affection are purring, kneading, rubbing, head butting, mutual grooming, and slow blinking.

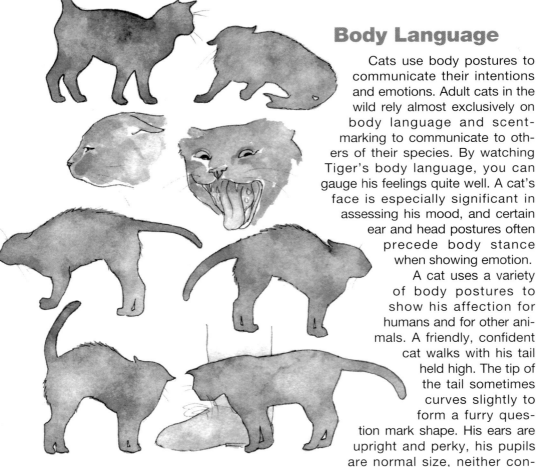

The cat's body language: (top left) friendly and confident, (top right) highly aggressive, (second left) fearful, (second right) defensive, (third left) aggressive, (third right) trying to intimidate, (bottom left) defensive, (bottom right) persuasive and affectionate.

In this food fight, the aggressor (right) swipes at the defender (left). If the less dominant cat doesn't withdraw, the exchange of blows may escalate into full-scale fighting.

• Kneading, a behavior left over from kittenhood, indicates that your cat feels a sense of well-being and emotional closeness.

• Head butts are another way of showing affection to other cats and to humans; Tiger leans or bumps his forehead against yours or another cat's to signal affection and social bonding.

• Mutual grooming is performed between close feline family members. If your cat tries to give you a bath, it's a compliment, not a comment on your hygiene (see Allogrooming, page 53).

• Slow blinks also indicate contentment and affection. Tiger stares at you with a relaxed, mellow expression, and then slowly narrows his eyes and opens them again.

• And then, of course, there's the cat smile. A cat being petted or sitting peacefully in a loved human's lap half closes his eyes and turns the corners of his mouth up in what can only be described as a look of extreme pleasure.

You'll learn to recognize these signs of affection as you get to know your cat and develop a close relationship with him.

Posturing

Cats will avoid fighting when they can, and they use a variety of body postures to signal their intentions. Most standoffs end peacefully after a "stare-down," in which the cats glare balefully at each other until the weaker of the two gives in and moves away. A direct stare is an insult to a cat. You might observe this behavior when two cats try to occupy the same sleeping area. The weaker will usually crouch defensively, leaning away from the stronger, raising the paw protectively, and, as soon as

The "U" shaped tail, slanted ears, bristled fur, and half-raised paw mean that this kitten feels threatened.

possible, retreating to allow the other cat to claim the spot. The standoff may or may not be accompanied by an exchange of swipes from their paws and growling or hissing. Usually, the stare is all that's needed to resolve the dispute.

If the defensive cat can't or won't retreat, or feels cornered or trapped, then the fight escalates. A frightened, defensive cat faced with a stronger opponent will assume one of two body postures. He will arch his back, turn his body sideways in relation to his attacker, bend his tail into an upside-down "U," and bristle his fur to give the impression of size and ferociousness. Or, he will crouch low, tail held close to the ground, ready to strike out if necessary. By assuming either of these postures, he is warning his opponent to back off, in essence saying,

"I don't want to fight but I will if you come closer."

You can tell a defensive cat by the position of his eyes and ears. The ears lie flat on the head and the eyes widen and dilate to give him the best vision possible. Unlike dogs that roll on their backs to signal submission to dominant members of their species, cats do not have a posture of submission; when a defensive cat rolls onto his back, he's freeing up all four feet to defend himself.

An aggressive, angry cat, on the other hand, presses the attack. He will approach stiffly, staring at his opponent and swishing his tail angrily. His movements are tense and slow. His ears twitch to the side to hear attacks from the rear and side. His pupils constrict. As aggression increases and the aggressive cat attacks, the ears quickly swivel and flatten until the backs of the ears are displayed. This is to protect the ears from damage. The fight is usually short, with the defender fleeing if he can. Only if two equally matched aggressors fight, such as intact toms defending their territory, will the battle be loud and prolonged and potentially perilous. The fight is usually preceded by loud menacing growls and screams of rage. The cats will stand their ground for several minutes, heads almost touching, growling and screaming their anger at each other. One tom will then leap at the other, trying to bite his neck. Both will roll over, each trying to get a grip on his opponent, raking and kicking with his back legs and gripping with his front ones. Finally, one cat will move into the role of defender and the fight will end. Losing a cat fight can have a profound effect on a cat. A cat that loses a territorial fight can lose confidence and become intimidated by other cats that used to be his equals.

Olfactory Language

If you've ever owned a cat, you know how much cats depend upon their sense of smell. Any new object or creature brought into the home, or back into the home after an absence, will immediately provoke Tiger to investigate the "intruder" with his nose. Any changes in the arrangement of his environment, such as rearrangement of the furniture, will also arouse Tiger's need to sniff each item until satisfied that the new arrangement meets with feline approval. Since cats are territorial animals, they pay close attention to their home environment. This also explains why minor changes in Tiger's environment can be very stressful for him. Even small changes in our households, trivial to us humans, can bring an enormous flood of olfactory stimuli to a cat.

For example, when you come home with your arms full of groceries, covered with the strange smells of the outside world, Tiger is right there to give the groceries— and you—a once-over. After a thorough sniff, he will rub up against you and your groceries. He is indeed displaying affection by rubbing you because he's happy you're home, but he is also marking you, and your groceries, as his personal property. We, in turn, reinforce the behavior by rewarding the affectionate rubbing and scent marking with returned affection and treats. During this rubbing, Tiger is also spreading your scent onto his fur so he can easily identify you as part of his family. Cats identify friends and foes more by scent than by sight. Fortunately, because of our inferior sense of smell, we can't smell the scent from a cat's scent glands, which is one of the reasons this form of scent marking is acceptable to most humans.

The scent glands at the gape of the mouth leave a distinctive odor on the chair, establishing this Blue Point Siamese's territory.

Rubbing

Rubbing is the most common form of marking behavior, although cats use scent marking in several ways to define and mark their property. Cats have scent glands on the temples, the upper lip, the gape of the mouth, the chin; around the eyes, the foot pads, the root of the tail; and in the anal region. These glands produce secretions, and when Tiger rubs up against objects, he leaves his scent on the objects. This is how cats mark their territory so they and other cats can identify it.

These glandular secretions give cats a wealth of personal information. When two cats are first introduced, they sniff each other on the head or under the tail, or both. By doing so, the cats gather information about gender, age, sexual status, attitude, and other data vital to establishing where each fits into the feline hierarchy. Two cats that are friendly with each other will often brush past each other, barely touching with only the side or tail; this is a casual scent greeting between friends.

When your cat stands in your lap and faces away from you with tail raised, he is giving you the chance to say hello and gather information, just as he would one of his feline friends. It's not clear what cats think when their human companions turn down this happy opportunity. In cat society, our refusal might be considered rude, akin to refusing to shake hands when meeting someone. Fortunately, cats seem to forgive our rude behavior, figuring, perhaps, that we're only human.

Scratching

A less accepted (by us) form of scent marking is scratching. When Tiger scratches the cat tree—or the new couch—he is also marking his territory. Scent glands on the underside of the paws leave the cat's personal marker on the scratched item, and the scratches serve as visual markers as well. Scratching also removes dead nail from the claws.

Spraying

Cats also use urine and feces as scent markers. The least pleasant form of scent marking is spraying, and this behavior has caused plenty of friction between humans and cats.

A cat spraying: This behavior is commonly seen in male cats, but both genders can spray. Altering usually eliminates this behavior.

Cats, particularly unaltered males but also unaltered females, will spray urine to mark their territory. Tiger backs up to a vertical surface, such as a tree or your new couch, raises his tail, and sprays urine onto the surface. He isn't being bad or spiteful when he does this, although cats have been known to use elimination as a form of human behavior modification. He's merely communicating to other cats that this is his territory. Even with our weak sense of smell, the intact male cat's urine smells terrible; the male cat has one of the strongest-smelling urines in the animal kingdom, and that's saying a lot.

Fortunately, neutering usually curbs this behavior, but spraying can also be a sign that a cat feels anxious or threatened, and even neutered males and spayed females have been known to spray if they are having a territorial dispute with another cat or a disturbance in their usual routine.

Cats, usually fastidious about their toilet habits, also sometimes leave their feces uncovered as a form of scent marking, to announce their presence and status. Uncovered feces are messages for intruding felines that this territory is taken, and that the cat is the dominant feline in the area.

Chapter Six

Developing a Bond with Your Cat

One cannot woo a cat after the fashion of the Conqueror. Courtesy, tact, patience are needed at every step.

—Agnes Repplier

The Human/Feline Bond

A recent television program on cats told viewers that cats see humans as cats, and that's why cats form bonds with humans. Personally, I think this theory gives cats far too little credit. Humans don't look, smell, or act anything like cats, and I find it hard to believe that cats fail to notice this. Cats are supreme observers; they watch everything that goes on around them. Cats know we are not cats, but they like us anyway.

Also, cats do not react to humans territorially; they don't try to run them out of their territory or react territorially to humans entering areas they have marked as theirs. In fact, cats mark humans as their property by rubbing against them. Some

experts believe that we are enough like cats to provoke bonding behavior, but different enough that we don't provoke territorial behavior.

Still, cat behavior is ingrained by millions of years of evolution, and much of the way cats behave toward humans parallels the way cats behave with each other. That's why learning why cats think the way they do is important, and why we must learn how cats communicate if we are to build a strong relationship with our cats.

It can't be denied, however, that cats can develop bonds with humans that are often stronger than the bonds they develop with members of their own species. Why do cats develop bonds with humans, a species very different from their own?

Some researchers believe that by nurturing and feeding cats, cat owners keep their feline friends in a state of perpetual kittenhood—in essence, keeping the cat from becoming an adult emotionally. Proponents of this theory point to the behaviors cats exhibit around humans that mimic the behaviors cats perform with their mothers: kneading on an owner's lap, purring, engaging in play, meowing at their owners for food, and so on. They note that the size difference between humans and cats is roughly comparable to that of mother and kittens, that when stroking a cat our hands are like a mother's tongue, and that cuddling into our laps is much like a kitten's cuddling with her mother.

On the other hand, opponents of this theory point out that cats also perform behaviors that indicate that cats think of humans as *their* children: They bring home prey, they groom their owners, they call to their owners as they would to their kittens. Cats also are capable of treating humans as they would adult feline friends: sitting together to enjoy each other's company, playing together, sleeping together. And what of the cats that make journeys, sometimes of hundreds of miles, to be reunited with human companions? Can this be explained as juvenile behavior?

The relationship between cat and human is not as clear-cut and simple as it might seem, and no one really knows what's going on in Fluffy's mind when she looks at her owner. It's dangerous, perhaps, to make generalizations about the human/feline bond, because for every rule there's an exception. Every bond is different, just as every human-to-human relationship is different. That cats treat humans as members of their families, however, is obvious, but who plays what role

The human/feline bond can be very strong and beneficial to human and cat alike.

seems to depend upon the cat and the owner.

Developing a bond with a cat—a true bond of affection and trust—is not a simple, quick, or effortless task. It takes patience, consistency, and a lot of TLC. The benefit of developing a bond with Fluffy is simple: The best way to keep your cat happy, healthy, and free from behavior problems is to develop a bond of trust and affection with her. Cats crave human interaction and companionship, and will respond to your love and affection with returned feelings. This bond is also necessary if you wish to train Fluffy to do anything. You can't get a cat to do what you want if she doesn't trust you. Cats will be motivated to please their owners only if a bond of trust and affection has been established.

Earning Trust

Cats are not like dogs; they are not genetically programmed for pack behavior. While you can develop a friendship with a dog fairly quickly, cultivating a friendship with a cat generally takes more time and effort. But it's certainly worth the trouble. In fact, some cat lovers mention this very fact when asked why their bond with their cat is so special. What we must work hard for is always seen as more valuable than what is given to us without effort on our part.

The first thing you must do in developing a bond is establish trust between you and Fluffy. How long this process takes and how successful you will be depend a great deal on a number of factors. Success depends primarily on your cat's nature. As any cat lover will tell you, cats are individuals and no two will react exactly the same way. They behave according to their unique temperaments. Their nature depends greatly on upbringing and early experiences with humans. You will have a much harder time establishing a trusting bond with a cat that has had negative experiences with humans in the past. That's not to say that you cannot develop a bond with a cat that's been neglected or abused (see page 79). Given enough time and patience, even semiferal cats can learn to trust humans—or at least a particular human who has taken the time to earn that trust. In general, however, you'll have better success bonding with and training a cat that's been well socialized early in life.

Choosing a Kitten

If you are about to acquire a kitten and you want to improve your chances of developing a strong emotional bond with her, consider a number of factors.

Temperament

If you are getting a kitten, consider the kitten's overall temperament. If possible, see the kittens when they are still with their littermates. Watch the entire litter for a few minutes. Tempt the kittens with a cat toy and see how they react. In any given litter you'll notice a range of behavior. You'll notice that some kittens are bold, while others prefer to hang back and check out the action from a safe distance.

A quiet moment shared by friends can be precious.

Look for a kitten that seems curious, friendly, intelligent, and used to handling. A little fear is normal and healthy, since you're a stranger to the kitten, but don't choose a kitten that cowers from your hand, runs away in terror, hisses, snarls, or struggles frantically to get away. Avoid a kitten that appears too passive or unresponsive. This could be a sign of health problems, temperament concerns, or lesser intelligence; yes, cats vary greatly in their mental facilities just as humans do.

Environment

Look at the environment carefully, too. Are the kittens allowed the run of the house? Or are they kept in a cage, away from human contact? If all the kittens in the litter seem unaccustomed to human contact, think about looking for another litter to choose from. Remember that the most crucial time in a cat's development and socialization is from two to five weeks of age. Lack of proper human handling during this sensitive period will affect the cat's ability to bond with humans to a greater or lesser degree. How much it will affect her depends on a number of factors, including inherited temperament traits.

Parents

If possible, observe the kitten's parents as well. Studies have proven that friendly male cats produce friendly offspring. The kittens exhibit the father's friendliness even when they themselves have had no contact with the father, indicating inherited rather than learned behavior. The reverse is also true; male cats that are unfriendly to humans are likely to have unfriendly offspring. It's often difficult to see the father, and if the mother is a free-roaming cat, often the father is unknown. However, if you can observe the father, or at least get a description of his temperament, you can better judge the potential sociability of the kittens. This advice applies when choosing both purebred and random-bred cats.

Observe the mother's temperament as well, since the mother's friendliness is also important. But remember that genetics is only one factor; environment plays a very important role as well. Observe the mother's treatment of the kittens and her relationship with them. An attentive, nurturing, and loving mother is more likely to have well-socialized kittens. Also, the mother's attitude toward humans will affect her offsprings' attitudes. A mother cat that's distrustful of humans may pass on that distrust to her kittens, since kittens learn by observation.

Breed

Breed, too, can affect how a cat will bond. If you'll be getting a purebred, before you buy talk to the breeder about the breed's overall temperament to see if it's a good match for you. One of the reasons for buying a purebred is that it is possible to get a pretty good idea what a given member of a cat breed will be like by examining its forebears and knowing the breed's characteristics. It is helpful to know a cat's temperament, conformation, grooming needs, and so on before investing time and money. A general breed book such as Barron's *Encyclopedia of Cat Breeds* can be useful in helping you select the right breed.

Keep in mind, however, that cats require effort on your part to become the best companions they can be. Just because a cat is a member of a breed that usually bonds with its humans doesn't mean that this member of the breed will give you its devotion if you ignore or abuse it. Cats will meet you halfway if you give them a chance, but you must earn their loyalty and trust in order to have the closest relationship possible.

Health

Look for a kitten that's healthy, happy, and alert. Health is just as important as temperament when it comes to establishing a bond with a cat.
• The kitten should be active and playful.
• The fur should be clean, soft, fluffy, and glossy, never dull or rough. Look at the roots of the fur. If you see tiny black particles clinging to the hairs, this indicates fleas. Fleas can be eradicated, of course, but you want a kitten that's been well cared for; parasites can indicate overall neglect.
• The eyes should be bright and clear and should not run.
• The face should not have tear-stains and the nose should be damp and cool to the touch.

• The kitten should not sneeze or wheeze, and the nose shouldn't run or be crusted with mucus, which could be a sign of respiratory problems or infections.
• The ears should be clean and free of dark-colored wax.
• The kitten shouldn't shake her head or scratch at her ears, which is an indication of infection or ear mites.
• The anus should be free of fecal matter or evidence of diarrhea.
• The kitten's gums and mouth should be pink, with no sign of inflammation, and the teeth should be clean and white. Gently pry open the mouth to check these.

Getting an Adult Cat

Getting an adult cat means you'll be missing the cute kitten stage, and you will also miss the early bonding years and the joys of watching the cat grow and develop. Also, you won't be sure that Fluffy was raised correctly and you will not know for certain that she received the proper care or socialization during that first year of life.

Kittenhood, however, is the shortest period of a cat's life and is soon over. If you're not looking forward to Fluffy's adult years, think hard before you get any cat. You'll enjoy the antics of the kitten, but you'll establish the lasting relationship with the adult cat.

Getting an adult cat has many benefits, and you can often tell if Fluffy is well socialized by her behavior toward you and toward her current owners. If you want a cat that will definitely be a lapcat, for example, you'll be able to judge that more easily in an adult than in a kitten; it's hard to judge exactly what a kitten will turn out like based on her kitten behavior.

Often, an adult cat has already been altered, saving you the expense. Kittens require almost constant supervision; adult cats generally require less training than kittens do. By getting an adult cat, you also miss the most destructive stages of Fluffy's life. If you are away all day, an adult cat will adapt to your schedule more readily and will be less likely to be destructive while you're away. Less energy is required to care for adult cats, and seniors and people with disabilities may find that an adult cat fits into their lifestyles more easily. If you have small children, an adult may be a better choice, since kittens are fragile and not as able to defend themselves against the sometimes boisterous attention of toddlers. Kittens are more likely to scratch or bite in self-defense than a well socialized adult cat.

Also, it's easier to place kittens than it is to place adult cats, so by adopting an adult you'll be saving a deserving cat from euthanasia. According to the American Humane Association's 1996 Shelter Census Survey, 71.2 percent of all cats entering shelters are euthanized.

Contact with cats and other animals has a therapeutic effect. Cats are used in pet-assisted therapy.

Many of these cats would make wonderful companions, but there just aren't enough homes for them all. Adopting a shelter cat is a caring and responsible way to get a feline friend.

If you decide to acquire an adult cat, you should look for the same temperament indications and signs of illness that you would look for in a kitten. In addition, you should look for signs of neglect and abuse and ask the owners why they are trying to find a home for the cat. If they seem too eager to be rid of her, it may be that she has a physical or behavioral problem that they aren't telling you about.

Keep in mind, too, that a cat may behave one way when confined to a cage and differently once you allow her to have the run of your home. Pooka, my rescued Siamese wannabe, was calm, sweet, and loving while she was confined to the "getting to know you" room (see page 100). Isolated from the other cats and not subjected to unfamiliar stimuli, she warmly greeted my husband and me when we spent time with her, sat in our laps purring, and was disarmingly well-behaved. Finally, our veterinarian gave us the all-clear on letting her mingle with the other cats.

When we let Pooka out, she immediately turned into the cat from hell. She tore around the house like a bullet, terrorized the other cats, clawed up the stereo speakers, and generally behaved as if she were possessed. Also, she no longer wanted anything to do with us humans. Fortunately, the period was short-lived. With love and consistent treatment she settled down and became our most affectionate and charming cat companion.

Note: It's always wise to isolate a new cat for at least two weeks and have her thoroughly checked and tested for feline AIDS (FIV), feline infectious peritonitis (FIP), and feline leukemia (FeLV) before introducing her to your household.

Building a Bond

Once you have acquired your cat, you'll want to begin building your bond of affection and mutual trust before you try to teach her to jump through hoops. In developing your bond, remember four things: consistency, affection, kindness, and patience.

Consistency is one of the most important things to remember when developing a bond with your cat. If you allow Fluffy to walk around on the dinner table one day and whack her for doing the same thing the next, she will be bewildered. Given enough inconsistent treatment, the cat's self-confidence will be damaged and she will become uncertain and anxious around you, not knowing how you expect her to behave. She can even become aggressive from fear. On the other hand, showing Fluffy that you can be counted upon to behave consistently and fairly will help her to trust you. Remember, you can't have a bond with a cat without trust.

Since cats are creatures of habit and love their routine, it's best to set a consistent time each day to groom, care for, and play with your cat. Providing consistent attention is vital when developing a bond. Spending regular time with her will cement your friendship, and you'll come to know the joy of having that warm, trusting relationship. Regular care benefits you, too. Researchers are now discovering that people who regularly spend time touching and talking with their pets have lower cholesterol levels, lower blood pressure, a greater chance of survival after heart surgery, and less depression and anxiety.

Your special time together needn't be hours, and it doesn't matter if the time is in the morning before work, an hour after you come home, or later in the evening. Fluffy will adapt to your schedule and come to anticipate the routine, even if your timetable doesn't exactly coincide with the time she would choose if she had a vote. However, early morning or evening is best, since cats are generally more active at dawn and dusk.

Think of ways to involve Fluffy in your daily activities. For example, several of my cats get informal grooming sessions each day in the morning while I'm getting ready for work. I keep their grooming supplies under the sink in the bathroom and, because they enjoy the attention, they follow me in. That way we all get our hair done at the same time, and it's easier to clean cat hair off the tile than off the couch and carpet.

Genuine affection is also vital when developing the bond. Cats are extremely sensitive and perceptive animals. Why is it that they seem to know where the cat lovers live and make a beeline for such folks when they are in need? Evidence does indicate that cats can tell cat lovers from cat loathers. For example, in a recent study by the Anthrozoology Institute at Southampton University in England, 8 cats were introduced to 16 men. Eight of the men liked cats and eight did not (men were chosen to eliminate preferences based on gender). During the four-minute intervals in which the cats were introduced to the men, the men were instructed not to speak or make gestures. They were allowed to move only their eyes. The cats ignored the men who disliked cats and approached the men who liked them, tails high and ears perked forward, exhibiting friendly cat body language. The study suggests that cats are able to tell who likes them without the benefit of overt body language, using only eye contact, subtle physical changes such as tension, and olfactory messages.

A friend of mine recently moved into a new apartment building, and was thinking of adopting a young cat that was hanging around her apartment, obviously abandoned by some former tenant. While she was considering taking the cat in, the cat made every effort to make friendly overtures and to dash into her apartment whenever the door opened. The day she decided not to adopt the cat, however, he abandoned his vigil at her door. She saw him only once afterward, and he completely ignored her. Somehow, he knew.

Maybe Fluffy can't read your mind, but she can read your body very well. You'll have much better luck establishing a bond with a cat you genuinely like. Cats can sense your feelings and will meet you halfway if you give them a chance.

Kindness, courtesy, and respect are also required in order to establish a bond with Fluffy. Cats love and obey humans who treat them well. To build the closest relationship possible, show her she can rely on you to behave acceptably. This means not holding her when she doesn't wish to be held (except, of course, during necessary duties such as claw clipping, pilling, and bathing), never hitting, shoving, throwing, or screaming at her, and providing her with diversion and attention. Some cats can even tell the difference between your laughing *at* them and laughing *with* them. If you offend your cat's natural dignity by teasing or making fun of her, you'll have more trouble getting her to trust you.

Patience is necessary as well. You may want Fluffy to sit on your lap, but picking her up and holding her there before she's ready for that level of closeness will alienate her rather than build your bond. Don't force yourself on your cat; allow her to set the pace of your relationship. Each cat has her own level of comfort when it comes to human interaction. Give her the time she needs to get to know and trust you and your bond will last a lifetime.

Playing with Your Cat

Don't underestimate the power of play. Even adult cats need to play, and playing will bring you closer together. I'm not talking about flinging a cat toy into the middle of the room and expecting Fluffy to entertain herself while you go fix dinner. Where's the challenge in attacking a limp, lifeless hunk of fabric? I'm talk-

ing about interactive play that will help cement the human/feline bond.

The benefits of play are many. Play helps keep your cat mentally and physically active. Obesity is a growing problem for pets, and an exercise program is as good for Fluffy as it is for you. It burns calories, maintains muscle tone, and improves circulation. It provides outlets for your cat's energy, so she is less likely to act aggressively, develop behavior problems, or climb the draperies. It gives an outlet to cats in multicat households, where tensions can develop. Play gives an alternative to aggressive acting out.

Play also relieves boredom, particularly for indoor-only cats. Keeping your cat indoors is the responsible thing to do when so many hazards exist for cats outside in today's world; however, special efforts must be made to keep an indoor cat entertained and stimulated. An indoor-only cat, left alone, can become bored, lonely, and depressed. Interactive play helps alleviate these feelings and can stimulate the release of endorphins, giving the cat a sense of well-being and self-esteem. Fluffy will associate these happy feelings with you, and this will bring you closer.

Cat Toys

Cat toys stimulate cats' hunting instincts, which they practice through play. My cats' favorite toys are soft foam rubber balls, available at pet supply stores for under $3. These are small and soft enough to be easily carried in the mouth, but not so small that they could be a choking hazard. They're good for games of fetch. Toys that look a bit like fishing poles are great for interactive play. These usually have feathers or streamers attached to a length of cord that dangles from a rod, and they simulate the movements and wing sounds of birds. Remember, however, to put these kinds of toys away when you're through playing because Fluffy might chew and swallow the string. The same goes for any toys with thread, string, yarn, elastic, streamers, or any other long, slender material. Laser beam cat toys are popular right now, but be careful not to shine the light directly into Fluffy's eyes since that can cause permanent eye damage. Also, these toys can frustrate your cat, because it's not possible to complete the chase with a victorious catch. Be sure to allow her to catch her prey; this releases the excitement built up by the hunt and gives your cat a feeling of achievement and triumph. Building Fluffy's self-confidence will make it easier to develop a bond. A self-assured and confident cat will handle stress more easily and will find it easier to trust you than a cat that's fearful and has no sense of control over her environment.

You don't need to spend a lot of money on cat toys, however. Sometimes the simplest toys are best. Cats make a game out of almost anything, and can spend time happily playing with a scrap of paper—if you're there with them to share the fun. You can also make inexpensive

Interactive play helps strengthen the bond between humans and cats.

cat toys easily. Stuff old tube socks with catnip and batting or, if you're into recycling, clothes dryer lint, but don't use dryer lint from wash loads in which you used fabric softeners or bleach. These toys don't even require sewing; just tie a knot in the end of the sock and you're ready to play. When the toy becomes soiled and the catnip no longer potent, simply unstuff the sock, toss it in the washer and dryer, and fill it again with fresh materials. My cats love this kind of toy; it's just the right size for grasping and kicking and they enjoy proudly dragging it around the house like freshly killed prey.

Be sure to recycle the toys, too, as cats become bored with the same old toys after a time. I keep toys in a box of catnip, and rotate them. When you bring out an old toy that Fluffy hasn't seen for a while, freshly scented with catnip, the toy will seem new again.

Grooming, Petting, and Massage

The physical contact of grooming, petting, and massaging is a great way to connect with your cat. It's as soothing for you as it is for Fluffy, and is physically beneficial for you both. After a hard day at work, sitting down and massaging, grooming, or stroking your cat will lower your blood pressure and soothe her as

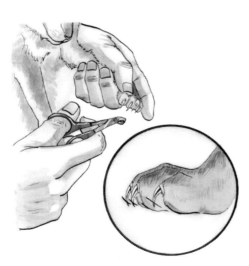

Press the pad of the foot gently to extend the claws before you clip. Clip the white area of the nail only, avoiding the pink quick that is rich with nerve endings.

well. You'll both end up feeling better for it, and your bond will strengthen.

Establish a grooming routine early in Fluffy's life. Preferably, you should start a grooming program when your cat is three months old. Grooming can be a pleasant experience for you and your cat if you train her to enjoy it when she is young so she knows what to expect. A regular grooming program is also good for a cat's health. Grooming removes dead hair that can form hair balls in a cat's stomach—as well as cover your couch—gets rid of dead skin and dander, stimulates the skin, tones muscles, and encourages blood circulation. It is also a good opportunity to examine your cat for developing health problems and attend to them in their early stages.

It's important for your cat to get used to being handled. Throughout Fluffy's life, there will be many times when you will have to administer care, and she must learn to accept your handling; otherwise, claw clipping, pilling, grooming, and other routine chores will be a trial for both of you. Acclimating your cat to being touched and handled is also necessary if you are to be successful in your training efforts.

How often you should groom Fluffy depends on her hair length and propensity to mat. Longhaired cats should be combed at least twice a week, depending on the texture, density, and length of coat; shorthaired cats should be brushed once a week. (Some purebred cats with long, thick hair, like the Persian and the Himalayan, require almost daily grooming.)

Choose a table or counter where you can easily groom your cat, or just go down to her level and groom her on the floor if she is more comfortable that way. Don't use a table or counter where she is normally not allowed. Not only will this confuse her, but putting her on a surface where she knows she's not supposed to be will make her uncomfortable and make the grooming session stressful instead of enjoyable.

If your cat doesn't enjoy being groomed, try to groom her for just a few minutes, and then move onto a more enjoyable activity such as petting and massaging. Gradually increase the grooming time until she is comfortable with it.

Petting and massaging come naturally to a cat—Mom's tongue massaged her when she was a kitten and you can take over from there. Massage can relax and revitalize your cat, and can be particularly helpful for senior cats that may have the usual aches and pains that age brings. Cats with chronic pain from arthritis, or joint, back, or hip problems also will benefit. In addition, your touch will communicate your affection to Fluffy and bring you closer together. You can also use massage and stroking as positive reinforcement for good behavior if your cat particularly enjoys her massage sessions. Stroking and massaging her will desensitize her to being touched, making it easier for you to perform routine care. It can

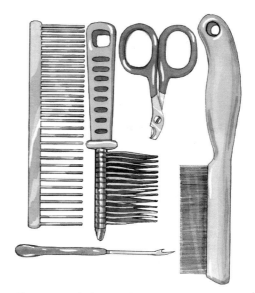

Recommended grooming tools include a good metal comb with wide and narrow teeth, dematting comb (if your cat is long-haired), flea comb, brushes, stitch ripper for removing mats, and nail clippers.

also calm a hyperactive cat and stimulate a bored or depressed one. Studies have even shown that massage can help the body heal itself and can benefit a cat recovering from surgery or illness. Even if massaging Fluffy seems a bit too "new age" for you, give it a try. The benefits for both of you are real.

Before beginning massage on a cat with a chronic health problem, check with your veterinarian to make sure massage won't aggravate your cat's condition. The key to effective massage is gentleness. Pressure that would feel good to you will be painful for your cat.

1. Begin with slow, gentle movements on the parts of the body where

Not all cats enjoy massage. Fluffy will let you know how she feels about it. Respect her wishes.

Purebred breeds like the Persian require almost daily grooming, so beginning a grooming program early in the cat's life is vital.

Fluffy is used to being touched: the back, head, neck, and tail. Don't stroke against the grain of her fur; always stroke in the direction of the lie of the coat.

2. Massage in a circular motion the muscles on the shoulders, the neck, on either side of the spine, and the hips, working down toward the tail. Remember to be very gentle when massaging the tail because the bones are delicate, particularly at the tip.

3. Don't forget the ears. Many cats love having their ears rubbed because their ears get itchy and it's hard for them to scratch them effectively. Take a flap of the ear between your thumb and forefinger and gently rub in a circular motion. Fluffy will let you know if she enjoys this or not.

4. Work down to the legs, then, if your cat will allow you, work on the belly area. Some cats are too ticklish for this kind of touching, but give it a try.

Allow Fluffy to set the length of the massage. You'll probably find that at first she won't understand the point of what you're doing, and may move away, bite your fingers, kick her feet, or think you're trying to play. She may also drop off to sleep.

You may discover sensitive spots that cause her to flinch; if you do, move on. Start with a few minutes of massage, and work up from there. You'll be able to tell by Fluffy's body language whether the massage is well received or not. Ecstatic purring will tell you that she is enjoying herself.

Bonding with an Abused or Neglected Cat

It's difficult for us true-blue cat lovers to face the fact that some people don't love cats as much as we do and neglect and even harm them. However, many cats face abuse and neglect every year and these cats need special care and handling to overcome their negative experiences. As cat rescue workers will tell you, working with abused or neglected cats and earning their trust can be a very rewarding experience. It's wonderful to see a fearful and mistrustful cat blossom into a loving companion when given the love and attention she needs. With patience, love, and understanding, an abused or neglected cat can become a wonderful pet.

You do need to realize, however, that developing a bond with a cat that has had unpleasant experiences with humans is a commitment on your part. It will require more patience and time than it would take to develop a bond with a cat that doesn't have the emotional baggage. Helping a cat regain her trust in humanity can take months or even years. Sometimes, a cat is so traumatized by her experiences with humans that it's not possible to make a connection with her at all. That depends upon the length and severity of the abuse or neglect, the extent of her injuries or emotional trauma, the age of the cat when the abuse began, and the cat's own personality and coping mechanisms.

Like people, cats react differently to stress, depending on genetic, environmental, and temperamental factors. Cats are extremely perceptive and sensitive animals and living in a violent environment, even when the violence is not directed at them, can have a profound influence on a cat's sense of safety and well-being. Generally speaking, however, most neglected and abused cats can be successfully reconditioned if given the attention and love they need.

Treatment and Care

An abused or neglected cat will react to the misuse in one of several ways. She may become fearful, withdrawn, depressed, or aggressive; sometimes, she will become all four. The first thing to do when you take in an abused or neglected cat is to schedule an appointment with your veterinarian, who can evaluate her physical condition and suggest possible treatment options for her individual level of trauma. If the cat behaves aggressively toward you, you may want to ask your veterinarian about a short run of anti-anxiety drugs. These can make it easier for an extremely stressed cat to adjust to her new environment. Antidepressants can help an extremely depressed cat cope with her new situation (see page 113).

Ultimately, however, it will be the care you give the cat that will turn her around. An abused or neglected cat has had her trust in humans

It will take time to win the trust of an abused cat. Be patient and gentle.

damaged or even shattered, so it's up to you to show her that you can be counted on to behave kindly and consistently. The same techniques you would use to establish a bond with any cat will work on an abused or neglected cat. You'll just need to be even more patient and help her work through any behavior problems associated with the abuse. If the cat spends the first two weeks hiding under the bed, don't try to drag her out and force her to interact with you. Move her food and water near the bed, and the litter box to a secluded corner so she doesn't have to go far to eat and relieve herself. Following are some important steps to take:

• If the cat is hand-shy and cringes from your touch, give her time and don't force yourself on her; allow her to progress at her own pace.

• Minimize changes in her environment during her first months with you. Allow her time to adjust to the routines, sounds, and smells of her new home. This is not a good time to decide to remodel the house or rearrange the furniture. Also, keep noise and confusion to a minimum, if you can, to allow the cat's frazzled nerves to heal.

• If she has behavior problems as the result of her neglect or abuse, you'll need to help her overcome them, but it's important to remember that these problems are likely the result of the cat's fear, anxiety, and lack of self-confidence. Use passive and displacement techniques to correct the behavior rather than scoldings or reprimands (see Chapter 8). Scolding the cat at this point is likely to make the behavior problems worse by increasing her anxiety and decreasing her self-confidence.

Goose, another cat dumped off at the park across the street from us, showed up in our front yard hungry, skinny, and apprehensive, but responded quickly to my friendly overtures and offers of food. Obviously once a house cat, Goose had an owner who cared enough about him at one time to have him neutered, but apparently not enough to keep him past middle age. Goose was docile and obliging from the start—a polite middle-aged gentleman, in fact. He didn't bite or scratch or attract my attention in any way if he could help it. He tiptoed around rooms, trying to blend in with the walls. I soon found that an out-stretched hand made him cringe and cower, and being picked up made him pant with terror. He expected cruelty—it was kindness that surprised him.

It took a full year of patient, gentle handling for Goose to accept being petted without flinching, and another six months for it to dawn on him that my husband and I weren't planning to do terrible things to him. Finally, his true personality started to emerge and his self-confidence returned. He'll never enjoy being held or be a lapcat, but he's a contented family member now, and I'm glad that we were able to show him some of the kindness he deserves. If you can open your home to a needy cat, do it. It's definitely worth the effort.

Chapter Seven
The Basics of Training

By and large, people who enjoy teaching animals to roll over will find themselves happier with a dog.

—Barbara Holland

Contrary to popular belief, cats are not too independent or dumb to be trained, but what is true is that cats can't be trained in the same way dogs can. Dogs respond to pack loyalty, and that's why dogs are much easier to train than cats. Once you establish yourself as the pack leader, the dog truly desires to please and obey you. That's the way their society works.

Cats, on the other hand, do not respond to pack loyalty, so establishing yourself as the dominant cat won't get you anywhere. Authoritative correction and negative reinforcement have no place in cat training. To a cat, correction is seen as aggression, which increases the cat's anxiety and reduces his self-confidence. That's likely to make behavior problems worse, not better, because uptight cats act out their anxiety in unpleasant (to us) ways, such as house soiling. The only thing a cat learns from punishment is to fear and avoid you as he would a dominant and aggressive member of his own species, and there goes your chance for a close, trusting relationship. Punishing Tiger may forever destroy your chances of bonding with him, and of teaching him to do anything you want him to do.

American writer Carl Van Vechten once said, "Cats seldom make mistakes and they never make the same mistake twice." That's a generalization so it's probably not entirely correct, but it is true that cats are extremely good at adapting and learning from their life experiences. Cats don't easily forget negative experiences, which is how they've survived. They quickly learn from positive experiences as well. If you make training a fun and pleasant activity, Tiger will respond with the desired behavior.

Why Train?

Why train your cat at all? Since cats can coexist with humans quite peacefully with minimal training, why bother? If you choose not to do extensive training with Tiger, you can still have a perfectly good relationship with him. However, some training is vital if you're going to live happily with your pet. For example, using the litter box and the scratching post are indispensable behaviors. Fortunately, these are easily learned.

But training has other benefits as well. Learning new behaviors stimulates the cat's mind and exercises his body. It relieves boredom and lethargy. Breaking away from the same old routine is a great stress reliever for both humans and cats and, like humans, cats enjoy a challenge and they like the feeling of accomplishment successfully learning tricks can produce. Training Tiger is also fun for you and can give you a better understanding of your cat and his nature. It can strengthen the mutual bond of trust and respect you have with him and is a great way for you to spend some quality time together.

Training Basics

At its most basic, behavior is a response to a stimulus. Cats, like all animals, constantly learn new behaviors we call *conditioned responses.* These learned behaviors are not based on the cat's instinctual responses but rather on his life experiences. For example, Tiger is performing a conditioned response when he dashes into the kitchen at the sound of a can being opened. He has learned that the stimulus (the sound) means food may be forthcoming, and responds with a learned behavior (he seeks the source of the sound) and is rewarded (he gets some food). Conditioned responses are used to train cats or any other animal.

Cats can be taught conditioned responses and they can also learn them on their own. My cats have learned with absolutely no prompting what the word "treat" means. It doesn't matter what tone of voice I use; they know the sound of the word, not the tone in which it is said. If I casually say, "I think I'll go get a

Cats readily learn tricks if properly motivated.

treat," a line of cats follows me into the kitchen. Treats better be forthcoming, too, or they stomp around the kitchen with their ears back, swatting at each other and complaining loudly.

Any cat owner will tell you that cats do just as much training of humans as humans do of cats, and probably more. When Tiger stands by his bowl and meows, and you reach for a can of cat food, he has taught you a behavior. You respond to the stimulus (your cat's exhibit of hunger) with a learned behavior (opening the can and feeding the cat), for which you are rewarded (he stops following you around the house screeching at the top of his lungs). Cats respond similarly to a system of rewards.

The principles of animal training were first defined around the turn of the century by Russian physiologist Ivan Pavlov (1849–1936), who discovered he could cause a dog to salivate in response to the stimulus of a bell if he first conditioned the dog to connect the stimulus with food. Conditioned response theory is also known as *Pavlovian* or *classical conditioning.*

American psychologist Burrhus Frederic Skinner (1904–1990) developed the second method of modifying behavior, called *operant conditioning.* B. F. Skinner was a strong supporter of a form of psychology called *behaviorism,* which views mental illness as maladaptive learned behaviors that can be unlearned. In his extinction principle, a behavior that is not reinforced will be extinguished or rendered inoperative. Conversely, behavior that is rewarded or reinforced will continue or become more frequent. In operant conditioning, an animal is rewarded or punished when it behaves in a certain way. For example, the behavior may be to push a lever. When the behavior is performed, the reinforcing reward, such as food, or punishment, such as an electric shock, is then given. Rewarding the animal increases the probability that it will repeat the action; punishment decreases the probability. It's this theory of positive and negative reinforcements that is most helpful in modifying the behavior of animals. However, in cat training, you'll be using remote or passive negative reinforcement (see page 85) and positive reinforcement only, as these will give you the best chance of success.

What Motivates a Cat

Understanding the underlying principles of training is important, but what is more important is to understand cat behavior and what motivates a cat to respond. Motivation is the key, because you will never, ever teach a cat to do something he doesn't really want to do. Cats are narcissists—you need to get them to think that performing the behavior is in their best interests. A system of rewards will motivate

Tiger to perform the desired responses.

So, what does motivate a cat? Primarily, cats are motivated by three drives.

1. Cats are motivated by their strong territorial instincts, because defending a cat's hunting area is necessary to survival (see page 38). This instinct is not much help when training Tiger. Offering him a larger territory if he will only roll over is not likely to succeed.

2. Cats are motivated by the sexual drive. Cats are efficient breeding machines, which is one of the reasons we have the cat overpopulation problem that we do. Unaltered cats, both male and female, are strongly motivated to seek out mates and complete the sex act. If not altered, they spend a good deal of their time finding partners, fighting off rivals, mating, and raising the subsequent offspring. This drive, obviously, isn't going to help you train your cat. In fact, it's downright counterproductive to training efforts, since it distracts Tiger from what you are trying to teach him. For reasons that will be covered in Chapter 8, you should spay and neuter your cats. It's the responsible thing to do and it will make Tiger a better and less frustrated companion.

3. Cats are motivated by food. Now, here's a drive we can harness for training purposes! Food rewards are the mainstays of cat training, and cats that are highly motivated by food tend to be easier to train than finicky cats.

Food rewards are the best tools for training cats.

Cats are also motivated by the desire for affection, but in a lesser way than the first three drives. Rewards of praise, petting, and other shows of affection are also an important part of cat training. Praising good behavior helps because if you have a bond with Tiger, he really does crave your affection and praise, but food is a much more important tool in cat training.

The Rules of the Trade

When training your cat, you need to exercise patience, consistency, persistence, and positive reinforcement. However, in conditioning some behaviors, such as scratching, *remote* or *passive negative reinforcements* can also be used effectively to eliminate unwanted behaviors. "Passive" means that Tiger will not connect you with the administration of the negative consequences of his actions. An example of passive negative reinforcement is putting bitter apple or Tabasco sauce on the leaves of your houseplants. The nasty taste discourages the behavior and the cat doesn't associate you with the correction. It's important for Tiger not to associate you with negative reinforcement, because that can damage your bond with him. Also, he will quickly learn that he can get away with the behavior when you're not around.

Rewards

If not handled properly, your cat can actually learn to do the opposite of the desired behavior you are trying to teach him. For example, if you are attempting to teach Tiger to come when his name is called, you must reward him for the behavior. If you reward him for coming on command by performing some unpleasant duty such as clipping his claws or poking nasty medicine down his throat, when you call his name, Tiger will quickly learn to run in the opposite direction as fast as his furry little paws can carry him. If, however, you reward him for coming on command with a favorite treat, with grooming—if your cat enjoys it—with a session of play, or just with some good old-fashioned petting and pampering, he will associate coming on command with pleasant things and will be more likely to respond. Consistency is the name of the game here; at the beginning you

must reinforce the behavior every time if you are to achieve the desired results. Cats don't work for free, and although cats can and do develop close, loving bonds with their human companions, that doesn't mean they are motivated to show their affection with unquestioning obedience.

You can also inadvertently reward your cat for undesirable behavior, so you have to watch what you do. For example, if Tiger wakes you up at 4:00 A.M. and you stagger out of bed and feed him, you have just taught him that waking you up at 4:00 A.M. is a good way to get food. The behavior will get *more* frequent, not *less*. Be aware of the messages you're sending.

In our home, Bitty loves to play fetch, and will bring her ball for me to throw. When she brings it back, she drops it just out of reach so I'll have to stand to get it. Requests for her to bring it closer result in a blank stare, but she always brings the ball right to my husband's feet—she's learned that he won't play this "reach for it" game. She knows I will, though. This is a perfect example of cat training in reverse. If you reach for the ball one time, your cat will remember. That's why consistency is so important in training.

Reinforcement Programs

While Tiger is learning a behavior, you will use *continuous reinforce-*

ment, which means you'll reward your cat every time he performs a trick correctly. Once he has mastered a behavior, however, and fully understands what he must do to obtain the treat, you will move to a reward pattern that's called *variable* or *intermittent* reinforcement. That means you will not reward him every time he performs the behavior. Rather, you'll reward him every other time, then every third time he performs correctly, then you'll vary the number of correct responses he must give before you reward him. Be sure to make it often enough to keep his interest. Remember, cats don't work for free. Intermittent reinforcement actually can be more effective at continuing behavior than continuous reinforcement. If you always reward a behavior over a period of time, and then fail to do so, a cat will quickly stop responding to your commands.

Extinction is the word for behaviors that end for lack of reinforcement. However, when you reward intermittently but still frequently enough that Tiger expects the reward, he learns that sometimes he will receive the reward. He remains motivated to perform the behavior in case this is the time for the payoff. (It's intermittent reinforcement, by the way, that keeps humans interested in gambling.) This reward system will depend on your cat, of course. Some cats must be rewarded every time, and all cats need to be rewarded often. You'll never be able to completely eliminate the treat reward.

Shaping Behavior

Extinction is sometimes combined with rewards to *shape* behaviors that are complicated or that must be learned in stages. For example, you may be trying to teach Tiger to come to you and sit at your feet. You begin by teaching him to come, and reward him for that behavior every time. After he really knows that he is expected to come, however, you begin teaching him to sit after he comes, and eventually you reward him only if he performs both behaviors. The behavior of merely coming will *extinct* itself, and the *combined* behavior of coming and sitting will replace it. Behavioral shaping is often used by professional animal trainers when teaching complex behavior.

Who Should You Train?

Have you ever heard the saying, "Can't teach an old dog new tricks"? Well, you *can* teach old cats new behaviors. Older cats can certainly learn, although younger cats will learn more quickly and eagerly than older cats that are set in their behavioral patterns. Also, younger cats have more energy for such nonsense; older cats are more likely to yawn and take a catnap.

The chronic health problems that can come with old age can also interfere with training. An older cat that has arthritis, for example, is not going to be enthusiastic about learning to roll over. Nor should you try to teach a cat with a chronic health problem tricks that might aggravate his condition. If Tiger has a health problem, consult your veterinarian before beginning a training program.

Not all cats are good candidates for all kinds of training, and you need to consider that when deciding what to teach your cat. Your choice of behaviors will depend on his personality and natural tendencies. For example, some cats naturally have a great tendency to carry objects in their mouths. It will be much easier to teach such a cat to fetch than a cat that never shows any interest in carrying objects.

Self-confident, curious, courageous cats will be able to learn more easily than timid, anxious, suspicious cats, and therefore the amount of socialization the cat has received is an important factor. A cat that has been abused or neglected is less likely to have the self-confidence and trust necessary to learn many tricks, but don't rule out a cat just because he is shy or has some emotional issues you must deal with. Since the training process should be fun and rewarding, training can be excellent therapy for timid or abused cats. The positive reinforcement and praise the cat will receive may be just what he needs to recover from his trauma. Don't rule out a cat because you've gotten him from a shelter, either. Many of the most famous trained cats have been rescued from shel-

ters. The cats that have played the character of Morris in the 9 Lives brand cat food commercials, and the Friskies Cat Team cats, have been rescued shelter cats.

And it goes without saying that intelligent cats will learn faster than less intelligent ones. All cats are individuals, and therefore your particular training experience will vary depending on Tiger's personality. Get to know your cat, and don't expect more from him than he can reasonably give. The primary purpose of training is to make your cat a better companion and to strengthen your bond, not to prepare him for a career in Hollywood.

Breeds and Training

Certain cat breeds are easier to train than others. Of course, a narrower range of behavior exists between the cat breeds than between the dog breeds. Dogs have been domesticated an estimated 16,000 years longer than cats, and the breeds have had more time to be selectively bred. The differences in size, qualities, abilities, personality, and so on are more obvious and extreme. With cats, the differences are less pronounced and, therefore, breeds of cats share many of the same behavioral traits. While all cats regardless of breed are capable of learning, your cat's breed can have some effect on your ability to train him. For example, if you want Tiger to speak on command, you'll have better luck with a Siamese whose natural tendencies lean toward

vocalization than you will with, say, a Chartreux that is naturally quiet. Also, some breeds and even cats with certain coat colors seem more easily trained than others. Tabbies are usually willing workers, and calicos and tortoiseshells have the reputations of being feisty and obstinate. Shorthairs are slightly easier to train because they tend to be more energetic than longhaired cats.

The Oriental breeds such as the Siamese, Balinese, Oriental Shorthair, Oriental Longhair, Colorpoint Shorthair, and Javanese tend to be more people-oriented and eager to please than other breeds, and are therefore usually good trainees. They also make good fetchers. Breeds such as the Ocicat, Tonkinese, Bengal, Burmese, Devon Rex, Egyptian Mau, Japanese Bobtail, Korat, and Turkish Angora are very

energetic and therefore are good training choices. However, cats that are extremely active such as the Abyssinian and the Cornish Rex can sometimes be more difficult to train because they can't sit still long enough to pay attention to you. Conversely, inactive breeds such as the Persian, Himalayan, and Exotic Shorthair sometimes can be too laid back to bother. Talk to your breeder about the breed's traits and tendencies. Even if your cat is a member of a breed that's not one of the best for training, however, he should still be able to be trained to some extent.

Training Methods

Not all cats can learn all tricks, and if you want your cat to perform a behavior consistently, you'll want to

The Tools of the Trade

To train your cat, you need the following basic tools:
- food rewards
- a spoon
- a clicker (see below)
- another unique sound maker
- a figure-eight cat harness and leash
- a cat carrier
- cat toys
- a spray bottle filled with cool water only
- other passive reinforcers as needed

work on that one behavior before moving onto another. Don't be afraid to teach Tiger new behaviors. Trainer Karen Payne of Miami, Florida, has taught her cat Princess Kitty to perform over 75 tricks! While your cat

Training tools: clicker, bell, whistle, leash and harness, special food rewards, a spoon, carrier, toys suitable for carrying, spray water bottle, hoop.

likely will not learn so many, and you likely won't have the time or desire to teach so many, your cat will certainly be able to learn some if not all of the behaviors mentioned in the following chapters.

When training your cat, the following techniques have proven their effectiveness. Professional trainers use similar techniques when training cats to perform in commercials, TV shows, and movies. They will work for you, too. You'll notice that in all cases, only positive reinforcement is used, and the positive reinforcement consistently used is food rewards. Dogs respond to verbal praise and petting as rewards for desired behavior. Cats enjoy praise and petting, but it's not a strong enough motivator for training purposes. They just will not consistently perform for such rewards. Remember, positive reinforcement is the only reinforcement you'll use. Punishment will get you nowhere.

Clicker Training

Clicker training is used by professional trainers and is an effective way to teach behaviors. It's also a wonderful and positive way to train because there's no negative reinforcement involved. Think of the sound of the clicker as a way of communicating with your cat. It's a bridge between the desired behavior and the reward—it tells Tiger that he's performed the trick correctly. Combined with positive reinforcement, this makes training Tiger an easier task, and certainly a kinder one.

A clicker is simply a piece of metal with a small indentation set in a plastic or metal housing that makes a clicking noise when you press on it. Clickers can be purchased from some pet supply stores and other specialty training stores. A clicker startup kit can be obtained from Sunshine Books (see Useful Addresses and Literature, page 156). If you can't locate a clicker, another sound-making device will work. It just has to be loud and unique enough to get Tiger's attention, but not so loud that it frightens him or so piercing that it annoys him. Toy "crickets" that can be found in some toy stores are ideal since the sound is almost the same. A retractable pen that makes a clicking sound will work, if it is loud enough. The sound must be one Tiger is not likely to hear outside of training sessions. That's why your voice is not a good attention-getting device—Tiger hears you talk too often and he will not be able to distinguish between training sounds and your usual day-to-day talks. Besides, the tone and timbre of your voice may change from day to day, and you want the sound to be consistent.

To begin clicker training, you must first establish a connection in your cat's mind between the clicker and the treat.

1. Take Tiger, the clicker, and a can or package of his favorite treats to a place with minimal distractions. Click the clicker and immediately give Tiger a treat by placing it on the floor.

2. Repeat this procedure until he begins to lose interest. What you are trying to accomplish is for him to connect the sound of the clicker with being rewarded. Repeat the program again the next day, and the next, until Tiger figures out that there's a connection between the click and the treat. You'll know this has happened when he begins to look for the treat as soon as he hears the click.

3. Now that Tiger has made the click-treat connection, you can begin to persuade him to perform certain behaviors for his click and treat. Be sure the connection is well established before you move onto the next stage. The specific behaviors will be covered in Chapters 9, 10, and 11. When clicker training, keep these tips in mind:

• The moment the cat does the desired behavior, click the clicker. The timing is very important; you want him to associate the clicker with the behavior. The wrong timing can reinforce the wrong behavior. Clicking too late is the most common training mistake.

• Avoid overclicking. Click the clicker once at the proper moment. Too much clicking will confuse him and render the sound ineffective.

• When Tiger has performed the behavior and heard the clicker, always reward him with a treat. You want him to associate the treat with the sound of the clicker and the behavior. Change the type of treat periodically, so he doesn't get tired of the reward. This will keep his enthusiasm alive.

• If you have trouble giving the treat and clicking the clicker at the same time, tape the clicker to the end of the spoon you are using to give the reward so that you can do both simultaneously. Some trainers use this method so they can hold the treat and the clicker in one hand, leaving one hand free for other things.

• When teaching Tiger a behavior, it's best to allow him to figure out what you expect him to do. Don't help him by positioning him yourself or trying to force him into position. That will hinder your progress, and he may become resistant to performing the trick.

• After you get Tiger to connect the trick and the click, add a word command. For example, if you are teaching him to sit, say the word *"Sit"* before he performs the behavior and gets the click and the treat.

• Once your cat learns how to learn—that is, understands how the game of trick, click, and reward works—you'll find that he is much more eager for the training sessions, has a longer attention span, and is more willing to learn new behaviors. Tiger will figure out that he can make the clicks, and therefore the food rewards, happen by doing certain things. If you decide you'd like to train your cat to perform on cue a behavior that he does often, keep the clicker nearby and click when he performs the correct behavior. Through trial and error Tiger will real-

ize what behavior is expected of him and repeat the behavior; then you can click and reward, and you are well on your way to adding another trick to your cat's repertoire.

• Stay on a consistent treat schedule until Tiger has mastered a trick completely. Then you can move onto the variable reinforcement schedule.

General Training Rules

• Your training sessions should be short; about 10 to 15 minutes is ideal. You don't want Tiger to become bored or annoyed by the training. Stop the training session while he is still interested, and he will look forward to the next session.

• A quiet place that is free of distractions is the best environment for training. A room away from other pets and people and without blaring TVs and radios will allow you and your cat to concentrate.

• Train Tiger when he is hungry. Right before his regular meal is an effective training time. If your cat has food available at all times, you may need to put him on a regular feeding schedule and pick up any leftover food as soon as he is finished eating. That way you'll have more control over when he is hungry.

• The above point doesn't mean to starve him beforehand, however. An extremely hungry cat will not learn quicker than a moderately hungry one, because he will not be able to concentrate on what you're trying to teach him. Extreme hunger will distract rather than motivate.

• Be persistent and consistent. You won't get the desired results by training Tiger once a month. Train him for a few minutes a day every day, but vary the time of day so he learns that the commands apply all the time, not just at a particular time of day.

• Don't give up if Tiger doesn't catch on right away. Cats are individuals and will respond differently to training—some will catch on quicker than others and some will be more enthusiastic than others.

• Use food rewards that your cat prizes highly. A piece of dry cat food from his bowl is not likely to produce an enthusiastic response; the treat must be something he gets rarely and likes a lot. A special treat such as a bite of minced meat baby food, a bite of tuna, a small piece of cheese, or a bit of your cat's favorite food is a good choice. Just be sure to make the treats small enough that Tiger doesn't want to go off in the corner and eat the treat at his leisure. It should be just a bite, enough to make Tiger want more. You'll be using a lot of treats and you don't want Tiger to fill up or become overweight from training rewards.

• Be consistent in your training techniques. Use the same commands, the same rewards, and the same signals every time, or your cat will be confused. Be sure your attitude and behavior are the same, too.

Training should be fun for both you and Tiger. With imagination and patience, the tricks your cat can learn are endless.

• Never hit or yell at your cat. If you find yourself becoming annoyed or frustrated, end the training session and try again later.

• Not all cats will be able to learn all behaviors. Your success will depend on your cat's individual traits. Don't hold it against him if you are unable to teach him a particular behavior.

• Remember that training should be enjoyable, not a chore. You'll have better success if you and your cat have fun.

Training Session Guidelines

• Always say your cat's name before the spoken command: *"Tiger, come!"*

• Teach only one behavior at a time; more will confuse your cat. When he has completely mastered one behavior, then you can move onto the next. You'll need to reinforce the first behavior to keep it fresh in Tiger's mind, but concentrate your active training efforts on only one behavior.

• After he does the trick correctly, reinforce the spoken command; you are trying to get Tiger to associate the command with the trick. For example, when he comes to you on command say, *"Come, good come."*

• Be sure to give him lots of praise and petting after the training session. Also praise and pet him when he correctly performs a trick for the first time.

• If your cat shows great reluctance to learn a particular trick, move onto another one. Don't try to pressure him to do behaviors he really doesn't want to do. Some cats are naturally more adept at some behaviors, and less adept at others. If the trick goes against your cat's nature, don't try to force the issue. Remember, you will never teach a cat to do something he doesn't want to do.

• Be sure to vary the location of the training sessions; otherwise, Tiger will learn to associate the reward with a particular area rather than with the trick itself.

• Once Tiger learns a trick, you must continue to reinforce it so he will remember. Refresh the training at least once a week.

• Be aware of your cat's body language. If Tiger becomes tired or annoyed, end the session and try again later. He must be in a receptive mood to learn well, and you don't want him to come to dread the training sessions.

• Your cat will gain self-confidence and enjoy the sessions more if he is successful. If Tiger just isn't getting a trick, you may be trying one that's too advanced for him, or you may be proceeding too quickly. Go back to a simpler one.

• Your success will vary from session to session. If one session goes particularly badly, don't panic. Everyone has off days, even cats. End the session and try again another day.

• Patience is paramount. Don't expect results overnight.

• End the training on a positive note, so he will be eager for the next session. Preferably, end the session after Tiger has performed the behavior correctly at least once.

Chapter Eight
Problem Behavior

It's very hard to be polite if you're a cat.

Anonymous

While cats generally get along well with their human companions, problems can arise because of the cat's inherent nature—and ours. Often, what seems like misbehavior to us is normal behavior for cats. For example, when unaltered male cats spray urine to mark their territory, that's normal behavior for them. Of course, that doesn't mean it's acceptable behavior to us.

Usually, behavior problems are an indication that Fluffy is trying to tell you something. She is not being bad or spiteful; she simply has a problem that needs to be resolved if you and she are to live happily together. With understanding, patience, and persistence, most problems can be solved to your and your cat's satisfaction.

Visit the Veterinarian

When Fluffy develops a behavior problem, your first step is to schedule an appointment with the veterinarian. Many health problems can cause behavioral changes, so you need to rule out illness before you try training the cat to stop the annoying, unacceptable behavior. Training will not affect behavior caused by medical conditions; first you must treat the illness.

Cats are very good at hiding signs of sickness, so Fluffy could be ill without your knowing. This is a survival instinct, since showing signs of weakness can make a cat more vulnerable to attack by predators. What might seem like misbehavior can be hidden physical distress. For example, if you're petting your normally calm and sweet kitty and she suddenly lashes out and claws you, it doesn't necessarily mean she is vicious and hates your guts. It could very well mean she's in pain and you touched a sensitive spot. If your cat urinates outside the box, she may have a urinary tract infection or even diabetes. If she will not stay off the dinner table and dives into your food every chance she gets, she could have a nutritional disorder that is causing

*The signs
of stress or
unresolved
conflict:
depression
and anxiety;
inappropriate
elimination;
compulsive
grooming;
aggression;
excessive fear
or panic.*

her to seek the nutrients she needs from inappropriate sources.

Check the Cat's Environment

If your veterinarian rules out a medical condition, look at what's happening in Fluffy's environment. Anxiety is one of the more common feline emotional problems, and it can create a number of behavior problems including house soiling, excessive grooming, aggression, hiding, yowling, and anorexia. Evidence indicates that cats experience feelings of anxiety in much the same way we do when faced with stressful situations. The causes of anxiety are many and when Fluffy develops a behavior problem, anxiety is often the cause. Also, some cats are just naturally more fearful than others, and minor stressors can have a greater impact on them.

Have you just brought home a new baby, spouse, or pet? Have you moved or changed the cat's environment? Have you recently changed your routine, gone back to work, for instance, after being at home all day? Even healthy cats can become stressed and anxious by seemingly minor household changes. Look at the situation from Fluffy's viewpoint and see what might be going on. Removing the cause of stress often ends the disturbing behavior. Keep a written record of what you observe and when you observe it to help keep track of your cat's behavior.

Sometimes cats develop behavior problems because they are bored. Cats need exercise, diversion, and stimulation, just as we do. A bored, lonely cat is more likely to act out with annoying behaviors. A cat left alone all day can become depressed. Be sure you are providing enough diversion for Fluffy.

It also could be that you are asking your cat for something she can't give you. You can't expect her to leave your couch alone if you haven't given her anything else to scratch on. You will never train a cat to abandon her natural behaviors. The fact that cats retain some of their wildness is one of the things that makes them attractive companions; they're free spirits that choose to share their lives with us. Therefore, we must work out compromises that allow Fluffy to express her natural behavior while allowing us to have reasonably nice furniture. By shaping the cat's natural behaviors using modification techniques, it's not necessary, as author and illustrator Missy Dizick advocates, to learn to like fringe.

Your veterinarian can eliminate the possibility of illness, diagnose behavioral problems, and suggest treatment options.

Overcrowding

Although dog-owning households outnumber cat-owning households, there are more cats owned (64.1 million) than dogs (63.8 million). That's because people who have cats tend to have more than one: 2.1 cats on average per household compared with 1.5 dogs, according to the American Humane Association. And of course having a companion for Fluffy is a good way to keep her from becoming lonely when you're off earning the cat food.

However, overcrowding—having too many cats for the space available—can create considerable stress for cats since they are territorial by nature. Many behavior problems arise from overcrowding, the most common being intercat aggression and fear aggression. Cats that feel threatened will defend themselves and their territory; therefore, think carefully before you take in that extra cat or you may find even your formerly well-behaved cats developing behavior problems. For cats to feel secure, they must have an area to call their own, one that is theirs alone and to which they can retreat. This is particularly true in indoor-only multicat households. Although many experts and cat lovers (this one included) advocate keeping cats indoors for their protection, keeping too many cats inside can cause problems. In their natural environment, when cats have a confrontation, the loser will leave the dominant

Too many cats in the same household can create stress and conflict. Be sure you have enough room for all your feline friends.

cat's territory, thereby avoiding conflict. But when both cats are indoors, the losing cat cannot get as far away from the dominant cat as she would like. Being forced to live in close proximity is foreign to a cat's nature.

In my hometown, authorities recently discovered a woman who was keeping 92 cats in an 11-foot (3.4-m) -long camping trailer. When investigators arrived, they were appalled at the living conditions of the poor animals. You can imagine how the place looked, but you can't imagine how it smelled! Not one cupboard, one surface, one corner of the trailer wasn't crowded with sickly, stressed out, starving cats. I sympathize with the desire to rescue cats from euthanasia, which is the reason the woman gave for keeping so many, but forcing cats to live in these unhealthy, overcrowded conditions is abuse.

Reducing Multicat Household Stress

Fortunately, as long as you don't have 92 of the tiny tigers, you can take steps that will reduce stress in multicat households. In general, you should not have so many cats that each can't have a special spot where she can go to be alone. Cats relish their privacy and need it to live happy lives. You definitely shouldn't have more cats than you have time and money to properly care for. Having many cats is expensive and time-consuming when you consider visits to the veterinarian, buying supplies, cleaning cat boxes, feeding, and watering, not to mention giving each cat the training, love, and attention she needs and deserves.

Another way to avoid infighting is to have your cats spayed and neutered, the earlier the better. Early altering will reduce the urge to fight and decrease the chances that the cats will develop territorial habits such as spraying (see page 108).

Making your house cat-friendly will also help. By creating an environment that cats can live with happily, you can often head off behavior problems before they begin.

• Create feline hideouts. Kitty condos with cubbies to which cats can retreat will make the cats feel safe. Cats instinctively head for a small enclosed place to hide when threatened. By giving your cats ample hiding places, you'll make them feel more secure. You needn't spend a lot of money to give them hideouts. A cardboard box with a hole cut in it is always a popular retreat for the feline crowd.

• Provide enough litter boxes for all your cats (see page 108).

• Leash-train (see page 124) your cats and give them periodic walks in the great outdoors.

• Create several feeding areas. This will allow the more timid cats access to food, even when the dominant cats are near.

• Cats lower on the cat hierarchy often miss out on feeding opportunities because of their fear of the dominant cats. Be aware of your cats' dominance structure and make sure that aggressive cats and cats likely to overeat are fed separately from the fearful or timid cats.

• Give the cats opportunities to see the world outside by installing window perches.

• Increase Fluffy's territorial range by adding levels. Cats enjoy climbing and feel more secure when they can view their territory from above, which is why they like to perch on tall things. It gives them a feeling of control over their environment. Tall cat trees or cat gyms and retreat cat shelving will go far to give them a feeling of increased territory and to help avoid conflicts. For under $50, I built a tall cat tree with two perches. I wrapped the posts with sisal rope, a favorite scratching material. Since I installed that cat tree and two other small scratching posts, my cats have kept their claws off my furniture. One friend of mine built sturdy shelving up one wall and all the way around the top of one bedroom to give her cats a raised highway for sightseeing and for a means of escape. Her cats love it. A screened patio or a screened cat enclosure with a connection to the house is also great for adding to the territorial range.

Adding a Second Cat

Another way to eliminate intercat aggression and behavior problems like spraying is to properly introduce cats to one another. If you are going to get two kittens, try to get them both at the same time. They'll play together when you're not around and continue to enjoy each other's company even when they're grown. Introducing a kitten to an adult cat shouldn't be too much of a problem if you introduce them correctly. Use

It's usually easier to introduce an adult cat to a new kitten, but conflicts may still arise. Feed the cats separately until they are used to each other.

the methods found in the following paragraphs for best results. After the adjustment period, they will usually settle their differences and learn to at least tolerate each other.

Introducing adult cats to one another is more challenging but certainly possible as long as you exercise care. Don't toss two adult cats into a room and expect them to sort things out; this will most likely make them hate each other forever. As with humans, the first impression is lasting. Patience is very important if you want a peaceful household. A recent study has shown that the first year is the most critical in the adjustment period. After that point, aggressive behavior usually tapers off as social relationships are formed between the cats.

Isolating the Newcomer

First, allow them time to get used to each other's scent and presence before introducing them. Put the new cat in a spare room that can be completely closed off from the rest of the house. Make the room as comfortable as possible and include a litter box, feeding area, and a retreat where she can hide when feeling insecure. Be sure this room is not the area your existing cat normally uses to eat or use her litter box. When you first bring the new cat home, put her in the isolation room and leave her alone to get used to the new environment. Spend some time with your existing cat to reassure her. Leave the carrier in which you brought home the new cat in an area where your existing cat will find it, so she can investigate the scent.

The time in isolation will allow your existing cat to smell the newcomer without being directly confronted with her. Be sure to isolate the cats for at least two weeks. An isolation period is necessary so your veterinarian can test the new cat for diseases such as feline leukemia and feline AIDS and make sure no incubating contagious diseases break out during the isolation period. If the new cat has parasites, this period will also give you a chance to get rid of them before introducing the new cat to the rest of your tribe. Be sure to pay plenty of attention to your existing cat during this time. The intruder will be threatening to Fluffy and she needs reassurance from you. At this point, be sure to interrupt your existing cat's schedule as little as possible in order to decrease her anxiety at having an intruder in her territory.

Introducing the Cats to Each Other

After the initial two-week period, if possible, put the new cat in a room with glass doors so your other cat can see and smell the new arrival without having to confront her directly. If you don't have a room with glass doors, erect a shield in the doorway. Two plastic baby-proof gates stacked one on top of the other is a good choice. Allow the cats to see and smell each other. Don't proceed to the next step until they are no longer posturing, hissing, growling, swatting at each other, and so on.

Next, put the new cat in her carrier and move it into another room. Leave the door of her old room open so your existing cat can investigate. Allow the new cat to investigate a room in which the existing cat has

spent time. After several hours, return the new cat to her isolation room. If all has gone well so far and the veterinarian has given the new cat a clean bill of health, the next day let the new cat out of her isolation room. Likely, she will slink around the house investigating. The existing cat may follow and hiss, growl, or chase the new cat. This is characteristic feline behavior and no need for alarm unless she attacks. An exchange of swats is not uncommon, but a full-blown fight must be prevented. Keep an eye on the action, but don't interfere unless they fight. Don't leave them alone together until you're sure they've declared a cease-fire.

If they do fight, don't try separating them with your bare hands. I learned this the hard way. In the heat of battle they may not recognize you as a friend and may bite or scratch. Throw a rug or big towel

First impressions are lasting; make introductions slowly and carefully. Adult cats can become friends if properly introduced.

101

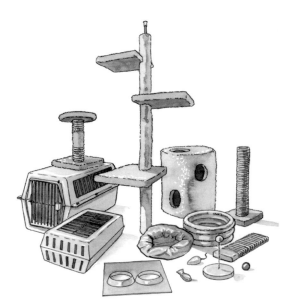

Necessary equipment for your cat includes scratching posts or trees, a carrier, food and water dishes, toys, and beds. Scratching equipment is vital unless you want your cat to exercise her natural urge to scratch on your furniture. Try a variety of materials and sizes.

though there's a new cat in the house, you still love her. The cats will usually come to an understanding. If they continue to fight and develop serious behavior problems such as house soiling, aggression, anxiety, depression, and so on due to the conflict, see your veterinarian for possible solutions and perhaps short-term medication (see page 113).

Destructive Scratching

Cats have an instinctive need to scratch, and no matter how hard you try you will not train Fluffy to stop scratching completely. It's unfair to expect a cat to curb this natural behavior. If no scratching post is available, your cat will satisfy her urge by shredding the couch, chairs, carpets, draperies, stereo speakers, and so on. Rather than punish her for the behavior, give her an acceptable outlet for her need to scratch. Cats also scratch because of boredom, and providing toys and diversions will help. Keeping Fluffy's nails clipped also minimizes the damage.

• Scratching equipment comes in a variety of styles, shapes, and price ranges, from simple scratching pads that lie on the floor or hang from a doorknob to elaborate carpet-covered skyscrapers. Let your pocketbook be your guide, but make sure the post has a sturdy base so it will not tip over and frighten Fluffy into scratching elsewhere.

between them, clap your hands, or squirt them with the water bottle. Put them in separate rooms as soon as you can do so safely. Check them both carefully for wounds.

The process will take time, but be patient. Until the cats have developed a workable relationship, continue to feed them in separate locations and keep a separate litter box for each one. Sometimes the dominant cat will prevent the other cat from eating or using the litter box. Shower both cats with affection and attention, and be sure the existing cat gets more attention than the newcomer. This will show the resident cat that even

• Carpeting is not a feline's favorite scratching material, so buy a cat post that provides other scratching surfaces as well. Sisal fiber rope is an excellent choice; so is natural bark. Again, your pocketbook and taste should guide you. A piece of scrap carpeting, turned with the jute backing facing up, makes a cheap alternative.

• Place the post near a sunny window or draft-free corner where Fluffy likes to spend time. If you put the post in an out-of-the-way place, Fluffy may shun it for a couch closer to her favorite human.

• Next you'll need to shape Fluffy's behavior: Extinct the behavior of scratching in inappropriate places and redirect it toward appropriate places (see page 87). When she begins scratching at a forbidden spot, give her a squirt with the water bottle. Be sure she doesn't see you do this, or she will simply scratch when you aren't around. You want her to associate the negative reinforcement with the forbidden area, not with you. When your cat uses the post correctly, praise her and give her a treat.

• If Fluffy ignores the post and continues scratching in inappropriate places, try rubbing the post with catnip or her favorite treat to make it more appealing. Make the problem areas less attractive by putting double-sided tape on the scratching areas and aluminum foil on the floor below the scratching area. Some cats dislike the feeling and sound of stepping on foil, and most cats hate

things that stick to their fur. Double-sided sticky tape used in carpet installation works well. A product called Sticky Paws, available at some pet supply stores, can help if double-sided tape isn't effective (see page 156). These nontoxic water-soluble acrylic adhesive strips are transparent and are applied directly to the furniture. They don't harm the fabric, and cats hate the sticky feel and will avoid scratching there in the

A squirt from a water bottle will discourage curtain climbing and other misbehavior. Be sure Fluffy associates the water with the misbehavior, not with you.

future, but almost any sticky substance that won't harm your furniture or your cat can be used. Your local hardware store may have just what you need.

• Also available are training devices that keep pets off forbidden areas by making annoying sounds or generating mild static shocks. They are also available at pet supply stores and through some pet supply catalogs (see Useful Addresses and Literature, page 156). The Scat Mat is one such product that produces a mild harmless shock and can be placed on the floor beside the furniture or over the scratched spot. These training devices work when you're not around to supervise the training. Buy one guaranteed safe for cats.

When given appropriate outlets for their natural scratching behavior, cats can be taught to leave the furniture alone.

• You can also try taping inflated balloons to the problem areas. When a cat pops one with her claws, the sound frightens her and she will avoid scratching there again.

Important: Only try this when you're home, so you can pick up the balloon pieces before Fluffy eats them. Swallowing the pieces can cause fatal intestinal blockages.

• Sometimes, you can resolve scratching-post avoidance by moving the post to a new location. Fluffy may not like the location if, for example, another cat has staked a claim to the area. By moving the post, or getting another one, you provide her with options. For example, Punkin had a bad habit of scratching the back of the couch, and all my efforts to teach her to use her scratching post were in vain. However, when I moved one of the posts to that corner of the couch, the problem solved itself. She continued to scratch at that spot but on the post instead of my furniture. When living with cats, compromise is necessary.

Declawing

Declawing cats to prevent them from causing damage is controversial. Some countries, such as Britain and Germany, have outlawed the practice as barbaric and cruel. Many American breeders, veterinarians, cat registries, and cat associations feel the same way. If you plan to show your cat, be aware that some cat organizations forbid declawed cats in both the purebred and household pet categories. Also, most purebred cat breeder contracts forbid declawing.

Declawing removes the germinal cells and some or all of the terminal bone in the toe, comparable to cutting off a human's fingers at the first joint. Usually only the front claws are removed, since they are the ones that cause the most damage to furniture and possessions. The surgery requires general anesthesia so the cat is subject to the risks anesthesia entails.

Declawing removes a cat's ability to defend herself and to climb to avoid attackers; therefore, declawed cats must always be kept inside. Some cat owners say they noticed personality changes in their cats, including failure to use the litter box appropriately, because of the pain after the surgery. Declawed cats reportedly have a greater tendency to bite as well, since they have no other way of defending themselves. Declawed cats, by the way, continue to scratch even though they no longer have claws and can still cause a certain amount of damage from repeated rubbing. Scratching behavior is innate.

Some people, however, feel that declawing is acceptable in some circumstances. As one veterinarian puts it, declawing a cat is probably less harmful than constantly badgering a cat whenever she tries to satisfy her normal urge to scratch. Since almost all cats can be taught to appropriately use scratching posts, make every effort to do so

A Seal Point Siamese wearing SoftPaws Nail Caps for cats. This is one of the painless alternatives to declawing.

before even thinking of resorting to surgical alteration. Keeping the cat's claws trimmed will also help minimize the damage she can inflict.

A product called SoftPaws Nail Caps for cats provides another option. These soft vinyl caps are applied over the cat's trimmed nails and held in place with adhesive, effectively blunting the claws and making damage to belongings impossible. The caps last until the nail grows out, about four to six weeks, and then are reapplied. Your veterinarian applies the first set and provides training in their application. The initial application and training costs around $35 to $40 and includes the first supply of the nail caps. From then on, you can do the application at home; the nail caps run about $18 to $20 for a supply of 30 nail caps, which is enough for three front-paw applications. Usage can be stopped whenever you wish. Nail caps are a positive, painless, and safe alternative to declawing. The nail tips are harmless even if swallowed, and come in several attractive decorator colors. See your veterinarian for more information. The product is also available in some mail order catalogs and from the Internet (see Useful Addresses and Literature, page 156).

Litter Box Problems

Litter box avoidance is one of the most frequent and irritating disagreements felines have with humans. Punishing a cat for inappropriate elimination will not solve the problem; it will teach her only to avoid you, and to eliminate when you're not around. Inappropriate urination or defecation means a cat is trying to tell you something, since cats use elimination as a kind of e-mail to get their feelings across. It's a sign that something is wrong. A new pet or person, a move or change in schedule, overcrowding, a conflict with another cat, or even a dirty litter box can cause Fluffy to eliminate inappropriately.

A friend of mine recently bought a new and expensive Persian rug, and immediately her cat began to urinate on it. The rug purchase happened to coincide with my friend's change in work schedule, when she went from a home-based business to a full-time away-from-home job. The cat associated the rug with her human's absence and, by marking the most recent environmental change, was trying to send a message—for her human to come home.

Cats that urinate or defecate on their owners' beds, clothes, or shoes are trying to send the same message. Cats use scent to attract other cats, and by marking an item that's strongly perfumed with their owners' scent, they are trying to bring their owners home. Cats are capable of punishing their owners—did you ever see Fluffy turn her back on you and pretend you're not there?—but in these situations cats are not trying to be spiteful. It's an attempt to communicate.

If Fluffy urinates or defecates outside the litter box, schedule an appointment with the veterinarian. Urinary tract infections and other illnesses can cause inappropriate urination. If the veterinarian rules out a physical problem, look at what's going on in the cat's life. Recognizing the reasons for litter box avoidance will help you find a solution. Watch carefully and discover when she is eliminating inappropriately and what is happening at the time. Keep a written record. Then try to resolve the situation that's stressing Fluffy.

Changing the Litter

A common reason for litter box avoidance is the cat's natural cleanliness. A dirty litter box can make her turn up her nose and look for a private corner to do her business. There's a good reason for this. Predators and dominant cats locate by scent; a dirty litter box makes cats nervous. Dominant cats leave their wastes uncovered to mark their territory. Try changing the litter more often; once a week is usually sufficient if you are using regular clay litter as long as you scoop out soiled litter and wastes daily. However, some cats aren't comfortable with that. You might try a clumping litter if Fluffy is particularly fussy. Clumping litters are favored by many cat lovers because the litter needs to be completely changed only rarely and remains odor free. The special granules of clay (sodium bentonite or attapulgite) make the urine form into easy-to-remove clumps. By scooping out the clumps and solid wastes daily, you can make all but the fussiest cats happy to use their litter boxes. Don't mix clumping and nonclumping litters.

Types of Litter

If a change in litter box behavior occurs after switching brands of litter, try changing back; Fluffy may not like the new litter. Some highly perfumed litters are offensive to some cats; other litters just don't have the right feel. Experiment with litters to see what she likes best. Buy a small bag of several different kinds. Test clumping or nonclumping clay (try the unscented); pellets of paper, grass, or corn cob; wood shavings, ground peanut shells, wheat, or citrus peel—the varieties are practically endless. Fill several boxes with different kinds and see which ones Fluffy uses most frequently. With all these choices you are bound to find one that suits her fancy.

If you are bringing a formerly outdoor cat indoors and she is not using the litter box, it could be that the litter is not what she's used to. Try filling the box with clean dirt or sand. Over the next few weeks, gradually mix the dirt with increasing amounts of the litter you want the cat to use.

Some cats do not like to share their litter box with other cats, and that can cause litter box avoidance. Provide one box for each cat. The size, shape, and depth of the box can also affect behavior. Some cats don't like the confining nature or increased odor of covered litter boxes, or feel trapped when using such a box. Older cats may have trouble stepping into boxes with high sides. Providing a variety of sizes and types may solve the problem.

Location of the Litter Box

Location, location, location, just as in real estate, is also vital to successful litter box training. If Fluffy doesn't like the litter box's placement, she may not use it. If you place it too close to her food and water dishes, she may avoid the box. Cats don't like to eat and eliminate in the same area. If the box is inconveniently located, for instance, down in the basement or on the top floor, Fluffy may find it too troublesome to get there. If the box is located so Fluffy has to brave some stressor to get there, such as the dominant cat's territory, she may look elsewhere to eliminate. Follow her and observe what's going on.

Put the litter box in an area that allows the cat privacy, but is convenient for her use, and accessible for cleaning. Some people prefer keeping the box in the bathroom, but in a multicat household that can get crowded. Since I have five litter boxes, I use the closet in a spare room, and I line the floor with sturdy plastic to make cleanup easier. An old rubber office floor protector goes in front of the boxes to cut down on tracking. My cats seem pleased with this arrangement. I also keep an extra box in the spare bathroom to avoid clashes; if a cat doesn't want to approach the boxes while another cat is there, she can slip into the bathroom to do her business. This eliminates problems if the need is urgent. For more on litter box training, see page 115.

Spraying

While it's more common for male cats to mark their territory, female cats also spray. This behavior is not connected to other litter box problems, because the reason for the behavior is completely different. It's easy to tell the difference between the two behaviors. When spraying, Fluffy backs up to a vertical surface, raises her tail and sprays urine onto the vertical surface, rather than crouching as she does during urination. Spaying and neutering (see page 109) will most likely eliminate this problem if you do it before the spraying becomes a habit. If a cat continues spraying after neutering, it can mean that the altering was not done soon enough, before the behavior became ingrained, or it can mean something is wrong. For example, even spayed or neutered cats may spray if another cat is threatening their territory.

Punishing a cat will not solve a spraying or house-soiling problem; it will only teach the cat to fear you and to eliminate when you're not around. Since cats locate their territory by scent, rubbing Fluffy's nose in the urine will only teach her that this is her territory and a good place to spray. Clean the area well with a non-ammonia-based cleaner and then block off the area so she no longer has access. Products that contain enzymes or bacteria for cleaning pet stains work by attacking the odor-causing bacteria and removing it, and are usually effective. It's important to remove all traces of the urine and feces or the scent will attract Fluffy back to the spot; but you need to address the problem's underlying cause to end the unacceptable behavior; otherwise, she will just move to another area to spray. Ask your veterinarian for advice if you're stumped for a solution.

Spaying and Neutering to Alter Behavior

Preventing unwanted pregnancy is the most important reason to spay or neuter cats, but altering has behavioral advantages as well and is important in eliminating unwanted behavior. Early altering means a cat won't display the restlessness, yowling, spraying, and other sexual behaviors inherent in unaltered cats. Altering benefits a cat's health as well; intact females have a seven times greater risk of mammary cancer than neutered females. Spaying also eliminates all uterine infections. Neutering males eliminates the danger of testicular cancer.

Neutering reduces aggressive behavior, particularly in males. If Tiger gets outside, he will be involved in fewer cat fights and will stay closer to home. Neutering's biggest benefit, though, is the reduction of the hormone levels that prompt spraying. Neuter your cat as early as possible, before the behaviors become lifelong habits. The risks are small compared to the benefits. Spaying and neutering are cheap compared to feeding, raising, providing veterinary care for, and finding good homes for progressive litters of kittens. Contrary to popular belief, altering will not make your cat fat and lazy; only too much food and too little exercise will do that. Nor will having one litter calm a female cat down. Cats usually need no such calming, anyway.

Spaying and neutering reduce the levels of hormones that lead to territorial spraying and fighting. Altered males get along better with one another.

The most important reason to alter Fluffy is that it's the responsible thing to do; you'll be doing the cat population a favor by preventing surplus kittens. If you love cats, you'll do your part to end their needless suffering. Millions of cats are euthanized in shelters each year because we don't have enough good homes for them all. It is vital that all cat owners—and dog owners, too—spay and neuter their pets. Even one unwanted litter is too many. Please, be a responsible pet owner and alter your cats.

Aggression

Aggression aimed at humans results from play or predatory behavior, or feelings of irritation or anger. Play aggression is usually caused by too-vigorous roughhousing when the kitten is young, or from overstimulation during play. If you or others in the household have encouraged scratching and biting when the kitten is small and cute, Fluffy may continue the behavior when she is big and this could be hazardous to your health. Cats can also play too rough due to being taken away from their mother and siblings too early, since they don't get the proper socialization that teaches them not to bite and claw too hard. Prevention is easier than correction, so don't roughhouse with your kittens because this teaches them that fingers and toes are cat toys.

Avoid rough play that may lead to play aggression. Learn your cat's body language so you can recognize signs of irritation.

If the behavior is already established, steps can be taken to curb it. Direct Fluffy's playful energy toward cat toys, and never use your fingers or toes or any other body part to tempt her into play. Another effective technique is to sit quietly with your hands in your lap. Fluffy will soon tire of trying to stare you down and will walk away.

Irritable aggression can occur when the cat becomes annoyed at some unwanted attention. This can happen when you're trying to pill, groom, clip her claws, or even merely pet her. Petting irritation is common; some cats enjoy petting only to a certain point and become annoyed if petting continues past their comfort level. Avoiding this kind of aggression is easy: Learn Fluffy's body language and if she shows signs of irritation or anger (see page 60), back off and leave her alone to calm down. Don't force contact or you may be bitten or scratched. Hitting or yelling at her will only make this behavior worse.

If Fluffy is so aroused that she follows you and attacks, defend yourself by putting a barrier between the two of you, such as a broom, rug, towel, or door—anything handy will do. Don't hit her, however, as this will be seen as an attack and will probably cause the cat to defend herself. Don't approach her again until she shows no aggressive signs. If Fluffy grooms, eats, or performs some other nonaggressive activity, it usually means she is calm enough to approach.

Redirected Aggression

Redirected or displaced aggression occurs when Fluffy is aroused but not able or willing to attack the real cause of her anger. For example, she may see a strange cat outside the window and react with territorial anger, but since she can't get at the strange cat and needs a release from the aggressive feelings, she runs over and whacks her innocent housemate or even you, her innocent owner. If Fluffy is angry because your dominant cat just cuffed her, she may dash over and cuff a cat lower down on the cat hierarchy. So, if she attacks you or another cat for what seems like no reason, the cause may be redirected aggression. There's not much you can do about redirected aggression except limit your cat's exposure to situations that cause her to react aggressively.

Compulsive Disorders

Compulsive behavior, also called stereotypic behavior or obsessive-compulsive disorder, is repeated behavior patterns that have no apparent purpose. It can take the form of excessive grooming, fixation on a particular object, yowling, pacing, self-mutilation, freezing and staring into space, and other such conduct. The key word is *excessive,* since most of these behaviors can be considered normal unless done in excess. This behavior corresponds to human compulsions such as excessive hand washing, hair pulling, repeatedly checking the locks on the doors and windows, and others. Compulsive behavior is often called *displacement behavior* because it is a mechanism for coping with stress or conflict. You've probably seen an example of displacement behavior in your own home: Fluffy, annoyed at being urged off a forbidden area, will stop to groom herself before stalking off. Displacement behavior can occur anytime a cat is placed in a situation where she feels anxiety or conflict. Displacement behavior becomes compulsive behavior when the cat is repeatedly put in stressful situations she cannot resolve and the behavior becomes so ingrained that it occurs even when she is not in conflict. At this point, she loses the ability to control the behavior.

Treatment for compulsive behavior is usually behavior modification combined with drug therapy. The first stop is the veterinarian's office to make sure there's no physical cause; a cat heavily infested with fleas, for example, may over-groom to rid herself of the discomfort. If no physical cause is found, you must find out what is bothering Fluffy so much that she has developed the compulsive behavior. Your veterinarian may be able to help you identify what is going on, because in each case the causes are different. If the environmental causes are removed, then behavior modification can often decrease or eliminate the behavior. In cases where the environmental cause can't be removed—another resident cat, for example, or your new room-mate—drug therapy can help ease Fluffy's anxiety and need for the stress-relieving behavior (see below).

Wool Sucking

Chewing on wool or other fabrics is a compulsive behavior more common in Siamese and Burmese cats than in other breeds or in random-bred cats, and therefore it's thought to have a genetic basis. Wool is generally the material preferred and the material is generally chewed with the molars. If wool isn't available, the cat will chew on other materials, sometimes even upholstery fabrics. It appears that wool chewing isn't caused by early weaning like other suckling behavior. Some experts believe that wool sucking is caused by the need for fiber in the diet, and therefore recommend feeding a high-fiber diet to help end the behavior. Giving the cat greenery and strips of beef jerky on which to chew may also help. If Fluffy consistently chews on a particular item, treating the material with hot sauce, Bitter Apple, or other topical chewing deterrent can help break the destructive cycle.

Eating Plants

Getting Fluffy to stop eating your plants is quite easy once you know the secret. It's best to curb this behavior as soon as possible because some houseplants are poisonous to cats. Usually, cats have good sense when it comes to avoiding poisonous plants, but indoor cats may munch on poisonous varieties because of the limited availability of edible greens.

The best way to protect your houseplants is to limit access by putting them on high shelves or hanging them from the ceiling. If this is not an option, passive negative reinforcement works well. Treat the edges of the leaves with Bitter Apple, which is available at pet supply stores or mail-order pet suppliers, or Tabasco or other hot sauce. The unpleasant taste will usually discourage munching. Keep the water bottle nearby and reinforce the lesson by giving Fluffy a brief squirt when you see her begin to nibble.

Since cats like to snack on greenery from time to time, you can often cut down on Fluffy's desire to munch the houseplants by providing a safe substitute such as oat grass, available from nurseries and in kits at some pet supply stores. Fresh catnip is also a hit with the feline crowd. Cover the potting soil in indoor planters with rock or fine mesh screening or Fluffy may use them as litter boxes.

Medicating Behavior Problems

When a cat becomes severely stressed because of an environmental change, has a conflict with another cat, becomes aggressive or extremely frightened, or develops a compulsive disorder, your veterinarian may be able to help with drug therapy. A number of anti-anxiety medications are available that can help get Fluffy through a rough period in her life, just as psychoactive drugs can benefit humans when we need help.

Veterinarians also have had good success treating anxiety and depression with drugs that increase the supply of *serotonin* to the brain. Researchers believe that serotonin shortages can cause depression and anxiety in humans and animals, and both respond to drugs that increase the brain's serotonin supply. Such drugs also work well on compulsive behavior such as wool sucking, excessive grooming, and *hyperesthesia,* a rare disorder in which the cat has sudden bouts of frantic racing, yowling, twitching, licking, and other bizarre behavior.

For example, Punkin and BigCat developed a sudden territorial dispute and were not only viciously attacking each other but were also spraying, even though both are spayed females. Behavior modification techniques alone had no effect. However, a short course of anti-anxiety medication plus added litter boxes and separate feeding areas eased their anxiety and aggression and helped smooth things over until they had worked out a territorial compromise.

This is not to say you should stuff pills down Fluffy for every perceived problem. While no medication will instantly cure all your cat's behavior issues, medications can influence feline behavior and help modify it. Combined with behavior modification, psychoactive medications can help her cope with situations that may seem overwhelming to her. Usually, drug therapy is used when behavior modification alone has failed. If your cat has a behavior problem that is not resolved by the usual methods, talk to your veterinarian about whether drug therapy can be beneficial. Not all cats will respond the same way to a drug, and sometimes several drugs will need to be tried to find one that's safe and effective for your cat.

Remember, never give Fluffy any mediation without your veterinarian's advice. Cat dosages differ greatly from human dosages, and dosages even vary from cat to cat—a 6-pound (2.7-kg) cat is going to need a much smaller dose than a 15-pound (6.8-kg) cat. Without a veterinarian's advice, you can overdose your cat. Also, some human medications are extremely toxic to cats; even "harmless" over-the-counter drugs, and even in small doses, can kill. One Tylenol tablet, for example, or any other drug containing acetaminophen, can kill your cat. Don't take chances.

Dealing with Cat Hair

Cat hair is not exactly a behavior problem, since cats don't consciously drop hair on everything you own and it's of course not possible to train a cat not to shed. Still, it's a fact of life and you must accept cat hair as one of the prices of cat ownership. However, you can take steps that will reduce the problem to a manageable level.

This is particularly important if you or a family member is allergic to cats. Cat hair is not what produces allergic symptoms in humans. It's an allergenic protein called *Fel d1,* secreted via saliva and sebaceous glands. Of course, when cats groom their fur, they spread Fel d1 onto their hair. Regular bathing reduces the Fel d1 covering the cat's fur and can reduce allergic symptoms, too.

Simply, the steps to curb the cat hair curse are: cover, vacuum, dust, comb, bathe, and train. Cover the most frequently used surfaces upon which Fluffy will sit or sleep. For example, if the cat bed isn't washable or is a bother to wash, put a piece of flannel sheet, a bit of washable blanket, or other such material in the bed to make cleaning up easy. The back of the couch seems a popular perching post for cats; cut down vacuuming time by covering the back of the couch with a washable "throw" or blanket. Beds are also problem areas, and cleanup can be made much easier by covering the comforter with a washable comforter, or duvet, cover so you can simply throw the cover into the wash with the sheets. They come in many decorator colors.

Grooming a cat regularly will go far in curbing the curse of the cat hair. In addition, regular vacuuming and dusting, as disagreeable as these chores are, will help reduce the amount of cat hair.

Train Fluffy to stay off the counters, kitchen table, couches, beds, and other areas you want kept clean of cat hair. Use the squirt bottle method: Fill a plastic squirt bottle with cool water and give her a brief squirt when she climbs onto a forbidden area. Be sure not to let the cat associate you with the unpleasant water. A training device that makes an annoying sound or generates a mild static shock also works well (see page 104).

Chapter Nine
Essential Behaviors

An anthropomorphic view of the cat is very common among owners, but this fosters misunderstanding. A cat should always be seen as a cat, not as a human being.
— Claudia Mertens and
Rosemarie Schar

Even if you choose not to train Tiger to jump through hoops, some training is necessary if he is to be a well-socialized, upstanding member of the family. Some of the following behaviors will interest you more than others, and of course you will decide which are important for your cat to learn. Personally, I don't much care if my cats tromp about on the counters as long as they know they aren't allowed to stick their noses into my food preparations or get near the hot stove. In general, all of the following behaviors will make Tiger a more acceptable family member. Read through the directions completely before beginning so you know the proper sequence of the training.

A variety of litter boxes and types of litter exist. Experiment until you know what your cat likes. Some cats don't like the confining nature of a covered pan. Litter pans should be cleaned regularly to encourage your cat to use them.

Litter Box Training

The first essential behavior is training Tiger to use the litter box. Fortunately, this is usually simple since cats are naturally clean animals and bury their wastes. Usually, all that's needed is showing him the litter box, preferably scented with a sample of his urine or feces. You can show your cat what to do by digging a small hole in the litter while he is watching. He'll get the idea.

1. If Tiger just isn't getting the idea, close off a small area—a bathroom or laundry room will do nicely—and put a clean litter box in one corner. At this stage, choose a litter box that's low and not covered by a plastic dome. Make sure the type of litter is acceptable to your cat (see page 107).

2. Place Tiger's food and water dishes in the other corner, and scatter toys around the rest of the space, since cats won't play or eat in the same place they eliminate. This will give the cat no other option than to seek the corner with the litter box in which to do his business.

3. Confine him to this area and observe him to make sure he's using the box appropriately.

Cats are individuals, and no one litter box is acceptable to all cats. Experiment to find what works for Tiger.

4. Keep the box very clean, but leave just a bit of feces and urine in the box because cats locate elimination spots by scent.

When Tiger gets the idea that the box is a good place to eliminate, you can increase the size of the area, but don't relocate the box yet. Open the door to the room but don't give him full access to the rest of the house, just another room or two. If he makes a mistake, don't punish him or rub his nose in the mess. In particular, don't swat him and then place him in the litter box! This will teach him to associate the litter box with punishment and he will avoid it. Clean the accident spot well and put Tiger's food dishes over the area. Place him back in the smaller area until he is using the litter box consistently and the behavior is well established. Now you can begin moving the box to its permanent location. Move the box a few feet every day until it's in the proper place, so that Tiger can keep track of the box and make the adjustment.

Teaching Your Cat His Name

The second thing to teach Tiger is his name. This is easy to do. Repeat the cat's name while engaging in pleasant activities such as petting or giving treats. Use his name every time you address him. At dinnertime, as you are opening a can or a sack of his favorite food, call his name:

"Dinner, Tiger!" Do this every time and he will quickly learn what his name means and to associate the word with agreeable activities, and he will be more likely to respond. Don't shout his name when he gets into something he shouldn't; a hand clap or squirt of water is better. You don't want him to associate his name with unpleasantness. Of course, cats can become temporarily deaf if they don't feel like responding, even when they know their names perfectly well.

Tolerating Touch

Since you'll need to handle your cat, it's vital that he be acclimated to being touched and picked up. He may not learn to like it, but you can teach him to tolerate it without too much fuss unless you have one of those rare cats that truly hates being handled. This training will be easier if you begin when Tiger is young. Make touching a pleasant experience first, before you try to stuff nasty medicine down his throat.

1. Offer Tiger a good-sized treat with one hand, a treat that he can't simply eat in a bite or two and run off. While he eats the treat, talk quietly to him and gently massage him with your other hand.

2. Repeat this every day, always offering the treat, until he learns to enjoy the massage, or at least accepts it calmly.

3. Be sure to acclimate Tiger to having his feet touched as well. This will

become very important when you need to do necessary maintenance on him (see below). Lift each foot up and massage it gently. When you're finished with the massage, give him another treat and praise him.

If Tiger hates to be picked up, you can try the same acclimation procedure:

1. Hold a small, very special treat in one hand and allow him to smell it.

2. When you have his interest, pick him up and offer him the treat in the palm of one hand. Don't try to hold him on his back since many cats dislike this, and he won't eat the treat in this position.

3. After he eats the treat, put him down *before* he begins struggling wildly. Praise him and give him another treat.

4. When Tiger learns to expect the treat and calmly submits to being picked up, allow a bit more time to pass before giving the treat, and then a bit more.

5. Carry him around the house, giving him small bites of the treat as you go. Do this every day and soon your cat will tolerate being held.

Tolerating Necessary Maintenance

After you get Tiger to tolerate being held, you are well on your way to getting him to tolerate necessary activities such as grooming, nail clipping, tooth brushing, and pilling. The

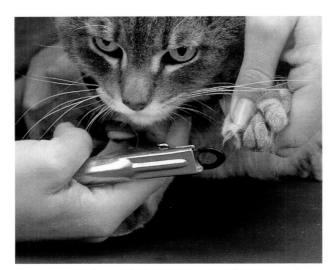

The less restraint used, the more cooperative your cat is likely to become. This cat is having his nails trimmed for the application of SoftPaws Nail Caps.

For example, BigCat takes daily medication for her medical conditions. In the past, pill time was a battle and I had to hold her wiggling body between my knees to get the pills down her throat. Then I tried some positive reinforcement with treats and praise after each pilling session. The real breakthrough came, however, when I reduced the amount of force I was using to get the deed done. Instead of holding her tightly, I allowed her room to move, and praised and treated her every time. Over the next few weeks, her panic and struggling ceased. Now I don't have to hold her in any way. I just sit beside her, open her mouth with one hand, pop in the pill with the other, then give her lots of praise. She doesn't enjoy pilling, but now that she knows I'm not going to hurt her, and she can get away whenever she wants to, she submits without trying to escape.

The same approach works well for claw clipping:

1. Try catching Tiger when he has just awakened from a catnap. Pet and praise him, then, without trying to hold or restrain him in any way, lift one paw and clip one nail. Praise him and give him a treat.

2. If he struggles to get away, allow him to go. Don't praise or treat him for running away, however; reward him only for permitting you to clip.

3. Try again after the next nap, and do another claw, allowing him to leave when he wants to and treating him if he stays. After a few weeks, he should allow you to clip his nails without too much fuss.

key to getting your cat to tolerate them is to use the *minimum force* necessary to get the job done. Most cats hate being restrained and forced to submit to anything, and will resist even when you're not trying to poke medicine down their throats. They like to feel in control, just as humans do.

Of course, restraint will probably be necessary at first, until Tiger learns that you're not trying to hurt him. Even then, some disliked activities such as nail clipping can become a battle of wills, but your cat will respond better if he feels he has some measure of control over the situation. While you will likely never get Tiger to raise his paw and smile while you clip his nails, you can train him to accept it with less panic and resistance.

The same method can be used for grooming, tooth brushing, and any other necessary maintenance you must perform on your cat. The object is to teach Tiger that he has control and that the reward is worth putting up with the disliked activity.

Staying Out of Forbidden Areas

Teaching a cat to stay off counters, tables, and furniture is not easy, but given the dangers that can be present on stovetop and sink board, and given the annoyance you feel when you find Tiger digging into the chicken you just placed on the table, it's best to train him to stay on the ground. Clicker training is of no help here; passive negative reinforcement (page 85) is usually required. Fortunately, cats respond quickly to passive negative reinforcement techniques. These techniques startle Tiger and are unpleasant, but will not cause him harm.

To keep your cat off counters, use double-sided sticky tape (see page 103). You can also booby-trap the area with coin-filled soda cans:

1. Fill each clean can with 15 to 20 pennies and tape the openings shut with masking or duct tape.

2. Set the cans on the counter edges so that they will fall over and make a startling noise when Tiger tries to jump onto the surface.

3. Make enough of these noise bombs so that he can't simply move down the counter a bit to jump up.

This technique will also work to keep cats off couches and chairs. The soda cans can be placed on the cushions so that they will fall over no matter where the cat jumps.

Aluminum foil also works for couches and chairs, but isn't as effective on counters because the foil doesn't crinkle as well on hard surfaces and therefore doesn't feel as unpleasant to him. However, sticky tape works well. Also very effective, if somewhat more costly, are the training devices that generate mild static shocks (see page 104). All of these techniques have the advantage of working when you are not around. And remember, Tiger has an instinctual desire to seek out high places. If he is not allowed on the furniture, be sure to give him someplace else to perch.

For table prowling, the squirt bottle method works well, as long as your aim is good enough that you don't end up soaking your guests or the food. Remember, for passive negative reinforcement to work, Tiger must connect the unpleasant consequences with the forbidden activity. If Tiger has already run off with half your dinner, squirting him will do no good at all. You must catch him in the act, and squirt the moment he jumps up on the table, so keep the water bottle handy at mealtimes.

Prevention is also necessary. If you want Tiger to stay out of your dinner, *never* feed him from the table

If you don't want Tiger's help with the cooking, train him to stay on the floor by using passive negative reinforcement.

or from your plate. If you do it even once, he will remember and will never leave you alone while you're eating. It's also not fair to give him inconsistent messages. If it's okay to eat off your plate one day and forbidden the next, your cat won't know what's expected of him. Consistency is the key to effective training.

Carrier Conditioning

Periodically, you'll need to take Tiger for a ride in the car, if only to the veterinarian's office for his yearly checkup, so you'll need to condition him in advance to accept being put in his carrier. It is likely that he has ridden in the carrier already, when you brought him home for the first time or when you took him to his first veterinarian's appointment. The carrier should be a sturdy plastic one with plenty of ventilation and a metal bar door that can be propped open.

1. Line the bottom of the carrier with an old, unwashed T-shirt that you have recently worn. That will scent the carrier with your comforting smell.

2. Place the carrier on the floor in an area where Tiger can see and smell it. Don't force him to approach it or try to draw his attention to it in any way. Your proximity may make him nervous if you've previously put him in the carrier. Allow Tiger to investigate it on his own. He will probably be wary but curious, and after investigating the carrier with his nose, he will probably leave it alone.

3. Put one of your cat's favorite treats a few feet in front of the carrier. Leave the carrier door open and, again, don't try to make him approach it. Allow him to find the treat on his own.

4. The next day, put another treat a bit closer to the door. Repeat this until the treat is in the carrier's doorway.

5. Continue placing the treat in the doorway until Tiger is comfortable eating the treat there, then place the treat just inside, and repeat. Eventually, you want him to be completely inside the carrier when he eats the treat. Don't venture too close while he is inside or he might think you are trying to trick him. And whatever you do, don't slam the door shut! That will undo all the good you've done. Let him eat and leave. Repeat until he is comfortable inside—you may even find him sleeping in it.

When Tiger is comfortable in the carrier, you are ready to take him for a ride. Be sure he has not just eaten or his stomach may become upset. Place him in the carrier—don't trick Tiger and trap him; just put him inside as you normally would—and take him for a short car ride. Don't drive him anyplace he doesn't like, such as to the veterinarian's office; just take a spin around the block and home again. Let him out of the carrier and praise and treat him. Repeat with slightly longer rides until Tiger no longer goes wild when you must drive him somewhere.

Coming When Called

You may have already taught Tiger this trick without knowing it, if he comes running to the sound of the treat sack being shaken or a can of cat food being opened. For this behavior, you'll want to use a sound maker other than the clicker, one that you'll use only for teaching your cat to come and that he won't hear at any other time. It could be a bell, a buzzer, a whistle, or any other unusual sound. For the sake of simplicity here, I'll call it a bell.

1. Every day for at least two weeks, sound the bell as you are putting Tiger's food dish down in front of him, then just leave him alone to enjoy his meal. This will start to establish a connection in his mind between the sound and the food, and will reinforce it two or three times a day, depending on your feeding schedule. If your cat free feeds, it would be better to switch him to a regular feeding schedule so you know when he is hungry and can count on him coming when you fill his bowl. If you can't change the schedule, however, ring the bell and offer a treat several times a day instead. Don't try to use the bell to call your cat yet; just allow him to make the connection. Be patient. Soon, Tiger will understand that the bell means dinnertime, but don't move onto the next step until at least two weeks have passed.

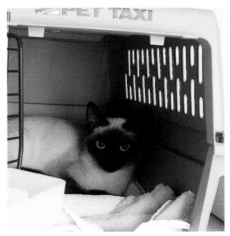

If you must travel with Tiger frequently, he will be more comfortable if he feels that the carrier is a safe haven for him.

2. At dinnertime, put Tiger in another room and close the door so he can't get to the feeding area. Have an assistant help you with this. Fix his food and put the dish in the normal feeding area. When the food is ready, begin ringing the bell. Your assistant should now open the door and let the cat out.

3. Continue to ring the bell periodically until Tiger gets to the dish. When he gets there, stop ringing the bell and say, *"Come, good come,"* then go away and leave him to eat in peace. Do this each day until your cat automatically comes to the food dish when he hears the bell. Be sure he is doing this dependably before moving on.

4. Next, change the location of the food reward; otherwise, Tiger will learn not to come to you, but rather to go to his food dish when he hears the bell. Go into the living room, for example, and ring the bell. He may go to his food dish at this point, but don't go to him. Just keep ringing the bell until he comes, and then give him a very special food treat and lots of praise.

5. Repeat, periodically changing your location, until Tiger is coming reliably. At this point, add the *come* command to the sound of the bell.

Chapter Ten
Useful Behaviors

The phrase "domestic cat" is an oxymoron.

—George Will

Now that Fluffy knows some basic behaviors, you can move onto other useful behaviors. The following tricks are not necessarily essential to your well-behaved cat, but they are certainly useful, and they can be fun, too. You'll be the talk of the neighborhood with a leash-trained cat at your side. Read through the directions completely before beginning training.

Using a Flush Toilet

The benefits of teaching Fluffy to use the toilet are obvious: no more messy cat litter tracked around the house, no more odor, no more expense for litter and accessories. The disadvantages are that you must always leave the lid up and, unless you can teach your cat to flush after each use, you and your guests will be faced with the results. Your more fastidious guests may not like the idea of sharing the facilities with your feline friend. Also, it's possible for the cat to miss her aim. Still, that's a small price to pay to avoid the drudgery of litter boxes, so if Fluffy will learn, this is a great trick to teach her. Keep in mind that not all cats are physically able or willing to do the balancing act necessary, and some cats will swear off altogether after being splashed with the rebound.

The best way to train your cat to use a flush toilet is to buy one of the training kits available at many pet supply stores. They aren't too expensive and if you follow the directions exactly, the success rate is good. It's possible to make your own form to fit over the toilet, but it will probably end up costing you about the same. The kit includes a plastic form that fits over the bowl but under the main ring and that contains attracting herbs.

A friend of mine had good success toilet training another way. First she moved the litter box into the bathroom, then she removed her toilet seat ring and fastened it securely

Before you take Fluffy outside on the leash, make sure she is used to walking with you.

to raise the box is very sturdy and secure, and doesn't cause the box to tilt or tip. And, of course, you really can't try this method unless you have two bathrooms and don't mind having one out of commission for a lengthy period.

Walking on a Lead

A real benefit to the indoor-only cat, teaching Fluffy to walk on a lead may not be as hard as you think, as long as you keep your expectations reasonable and don't expect her to heel as a dog would. It's more accurate to say that your cat will walk you. The advantages to lead training are that you can take Fluffy outdoors without fear of her getting run over or vanishing into the night and you and your cat will benefit from the fresh air and sunshine.

Some cats and some situations contraindicate leash training. Timid, easily frightened cats should not be walked anywhere but the safety of your own fenced yard, and only then if they show themselves capable of handling the situation without panicking. If you live in a city, I wouldn't recommend trying to walk Fluffy where so many frightening and dangerous situations exist. If she panics while you are out walking, you will have a terrible time getting her—and you—home in one piece. If you pick up Fluffy, she will likely hurt you. If you allow her to struggle at the end of the leash, she will likely hurt herself, and may escape and be run

over the litter box, so the cat got used to the ring idea. After the cat was using the box reliably, she put aluminum foil over the cat litter to encourage her cat to stand on the ring, leaving a hole in the middle so her cat could still see and smell the litter. Next, she put the box on a piece of wood so it was slightly raised. Over the next month, she raised the box higher and higher until it was level with the toilet. She moved it closer and closer to the toilet until the two were touching. Finally, she removed the litter box and reattached the toilet seat to the toilet, placing aluminum foil under the seat. Finally, she removed the foil and her cat continued to use the toilet.

The key to this method is attaching the ring to the litter box securely, because if the cat slips off, she will likely avoid the ring from then on. Also be sure that the base you use over or vanish forever. Walk Fluffy only if you have an environment that is safe and free of real and (to your cat) perceived dangers.

If your cat is an indoor-only cat and learns to love the outdoors, she may badger you for walks, and may even try for unsupervised strolls. One of my friends leash-trained her cat and forever after had to dart in and out of doors to keep the cat from escaping.

1. Get the proper equipment. The proper harness has one strap that passes around Fluffy's neck and another that passes behind the forelegs around her middle. You want a good-quality one—light, strong, and with a sturdy metal buckle and a metal ring in the center of the harness to allow you to attach the leash. Be sure to get the correct size; the harness should be snug but not so tight that it chokes your cat. A standard collar is not appropriate for leash training or walking because a cat's neck is much more fragile than a dog's. Also, some cats can wiggle free from such collars. *Never* use a choke chain or any kind of correction collar made for dogs; they can break Fluffy's neck and it's too easy for her to escape from them.

The leash should be strong, lightweight nylon, no longer than 6 feet (1.8 m), with a metal clip at one end and a sturdy loop at the other for your wrist so if Fluffy makes a break for it, you won't lose your grip. Also, you want Fluffy close enough so if a dog or other danger approaches, you can quickly pick her up.

2. Get Fluffy used to her figure-eight harness. Put the harness on loosely without the leash attached, and give her a treat to distract her. She may wiggle, bite at the harness, fall over, or lie down. That's okay. Leave the harness on for ten minutes, then remove it and give your cat lots of praise and a treat. Repeat this twice a day, offering a treat when you put it on and take it off. Don't leave the cat unattended in the harness.

Cats don't heel the way dogs do; allow Fluffy to investigate the outdoors at her own pace.

3. When Fluffy doesn't freak out when wearing the harness, fasten it more tightly and encourage her to walk around by kneeling several feet away and offering a treat. If she walks to you, praise her and give her the treat. Gradually kneel farther away.

4. Once Fluffy accepts the harness, give her a treat, attach the leash, and allow her to drag it around the house. Do this each day for a few minutes at a time. Always treat and praise. Don't try to lead her at this point; just allow the cat to get used to the feeling of the leash. Keep an eye on your cat at all times so she doesn't get hung up somewhere. Gradually increase the time.

5. Pick up the leash and walk with your cat indoors. Don't try to drag her around or lead her anywhere; allow her to go where she wants. Give treats and praise whenever she walks calmly. If she struggles to get away, you are likely not allowing her

enough freedom to go where she wants.

6. When Fluffy has accepted the concept of walking with you, you are ready to take her outside. Your first session should be for a few minutes only in a protected area such as your fenced backyard. Don't take her to a place where she might be confronted by other animals, people, or frightening noises. If this is Fluffy's first visit outside, be extra careful; just step outside the door and set her down for a minute or two. If she reacts with curiosity rather than fear, you can gradually increase the time you spend outside.

Sitting

This trick is an important one to learn if you plan on teaching more advanced tricks. For example, *sit* should be taught before trying *stand* or *wave.* Sitting is also handy when you need Fluffy to sit for some necessary maintenance. You will need a spoon and a clicker for this training.

1. Put Fluffy on a raised surface so she is easy to reach, but don't use a place usually forbidden to her. Put a bit of yummy food treat, such as baby food or tuna, on a spoon and be sure she sees and smells the food so you have her attention.

2. Say, *"Fluffy, sit,"* and at the same moment move the spoon over her head so she has to tilt her head up to see the food. Her natural reaction to this will be to sit so she can keep her balance and continue to see the treat.

Move the spoon with the treat over Fluffy's head; she should sit as you do so.

The spoon should be just an inch or two above Fluffy's head or she may stand up to reach it, and it must be over the cat's head or she will move forward to get the food. If she doesn't sit, withdraw the food and try again. And again. If Fluffy simply refuses, stop and try again later. She may not be hungry enough.

3. When the cat sits, click the clicker, say, *"Sit, good sit,"* and immediately give the food reward. It's very important to click the clicker at the exact moment the cat sits to reinforce the right behavior. Practice several times a day.

4. Eventually, in a week or two, Fluffy will figure out what is expected of her and will sit when she hears the verbal command. When she is sitting consistently, try saying *"Sit"* without the food reward to see if she really understands what the command means. If not, more practice is in order. If she does sit, click the clicker, wait a moment, and then give the treat and lots of praise and petting. Practice.

5. Change the location of the trick, so Fluffy knows that *"Sit"* means *sit* wherever she happens to be and not just in the special training area. Continue to practice using the intermittent reinforcement schedule (see page 86).

Staying

When Fluffy has mastered the *sit* command, move naturally onto the *stay.* The *stay* is enormously helpful when you are trying to teach your cat new tricks and when you are grooming her or giving her necessary maintenance. Your goal is for her to stay in position until you release her. This means that she must continue to pay attention and not wander off, stare at the wall, or curl up for a nap; therefore, make sure you are in an area with no distractions. Also, if Fluffy is too hungry, she might not sit still while the food is in front of her, so practice this trick after mealtimes, not before.

1. Put Fluffy on a raised surface and tell her to sit. Make sure she has room to move forward; if she has no choice but to stay put or plunge off the edge, she won't get the idea that you want her to stay. After your cat sits, say, *"Fluffy, stay,"* and gently press two fingers against her forehead. Take a step back. If she stays even for a few seconds, reward her and say, *"Stay, good stay."* If she

This cat is obviously enjoying the training. End the session while your cat is still enthusiastic.

Press two fingers against Fluffy's fore-head while giving the stay *command.*

immediately gets up, don't offer the reward. Start over, this time keeping your fingers on her forehead while you step back. Reward and praise any correct response. Practice several times a day for at least two weeks.

2. When Fluffy has gotten the idea, you can begin to step back farther, but continue to give the verbal command and make the two-finger gesture. In this case, the gesture is as important as the verbal command. If she gets up, wanders off, lies down, or does anything other than sit and watch you, go back to the last step, repeat the *stay* command, and reinforce the behavior before moving away again.

3. Gradually increase your distance away, and the amount of time Fluffy must stay to get the reward. If she gets up at any time, don't reward or punish; just go back to Step 2 and practice. Always release her from the *stay* with a consistent verbal cue such as *"Okay"* or *"Good Fluffy!"*

4. When your cat knows the stay command well, change locations and arrange distractions for her. Have the TV on behind her, or your other cats in the room. Have someone ring the doorbell. Be sure she has the trick well in hand before you do anything too tempting, such as tossing a cat toy across the room. Fluffy should get to the point where she understands she must stay until you release her, no matter what is going on around her. Continue to practice using the intermittent reinforcement schedule.

Standing

In this case, *stand* means standing on all fours, not standing on the hind legs. This is useful when the cat must stand for a period during grooming or in the veterinarian's office. (If your cat responds to your commands while at the veterinarian's, you know Fluffy is *really* well trained.)

1. Begin with your cat sitting on a raised surface. Have a clicker and treats on hand. Say *"Fluffy, stand,"* while scratching or rubbing her back at the base of the tail. This will cause almost any cat to raise the hind end in response. As soon as she stands, click the clicker, offer the reward, and say, *"Stand, good stand!"* Repeat several times each day.

2. When your cat automatically stands when you give the verbal command, cease caressing her back each time, but still click and reward. Continue to practice.

3. When Fluffy knows the command well, test her understanding by giving the command without holding the treat ready. If she stands, you know she has made the connection.

4. Change the location of the trick so that Fluffy knows that the command applies to all locations. Continue to practice, using the intermittent reinforcement schedule (see page 86).

5. Along with the *sit* command, now you can add the *stay* command to your cat's repertoire.

Scratching or rubbing Fluffy at the base of the tail will make her stand up. Immediately click the clicker and offer the treat.

Preparing for the Show Ring

Usually, at some time during cat ownership, the thought of showing cats comes to mind. Whether you have a purebred or a random-bred cat, you can enter Fluffy in competition. Some people show their cats occasionally whenever a cat show comes to town, and consider showing their cat a pleasing hobby where they meet with friends and talk cat. Other exhibitors take showing their cats very seriously and make promoting and advancing their cats full-time jobs. Whatever approach you choose, you will find like-minded folks in the show halls. Showing your cat, whether in the purebred or household pet category, can be an exciting, fun, and rewarding experience. It also can be expensive,

exhausting, time-consuming, and disappointing if your beloved cat companion, whom you think is beautiful beyond words, is not chosen by the judges.

Before you decide to show, be sure to take in a few cat shows so you can become familiar with the process. Several good books on showing are available (see Useful Addresses and Literature, page 158) and can help you decide if showing is for you and your cat.

Fluffy must be prepared for the process well in advance. The noise, commotion, and handling she will get when being shown can be very upsetting to an unprepared cat. Your cat's mental readiness is just as important as her grooming. If Fluffy has never been shown, prepare her ahead of time, or you may have a seriously panicked cat on your hands. A cat that bites or scratches

At American cat shows, the cats are removed from the holding cages one by one and evaluated by the judge.

Fluffy must be accustomed to handling to be successful in the show ring.

the judge, or struggles frantically to get away, won't make a favorable impression.

1. Get Fluffy used to being confined in the benching cage by keeping her caged for short periods at home, since she will spend most of her time in the cage at the cat show. She'll fare better if she's familiar with the process. Special cages can be purchased at pet supply stores.

2. Accustom her to being handled by strangers. Well before the show, have several friends come over and pretend to judge her. Be sure she is not familiar with these friends. Have them hold her up, stretch her out, run a hand through her fur, and wave a feather in front of her nose to test her reaction.

If she reacts badly or runs from your friends, you'll need to acclimate Fluffy by beginning slowly. First have

a friend—we'll call him Joe—just come into the room while you pet and reassure Fluffy. When she behaves well and remains calm, offer a treat and lots of praise. Then have Joe come closer, until he is standing beside your cat. Reward and praise until Fluffy accepts this. Next, have Joe pet her. Finally, have him lift and carry her.

3. Get Fluffy used to traveling (see page 120). If you decide to show, it's vital that your cat travel well, since showing often requires lengthy car or even plane travel. Take it slowly and your cat may even learn to enjoy riding in the car.

4. When Fluffy seems ready, enter her in her first cat show. The first show should be close by, so if your cat can't handle the commotion, you won't have far to go to get her home to safety.

Chapter Eleven

Just for Fun

There is nothing in the animal world, to my mind, more delightful than grown cats at play. They are so swift and light and graceful, so subtle and designing, and yet so richly comic.

—Monica Edwards

Training Tiger shouldn't be a chore. Following are a few tricks you can teach him just for fun. If he has shown aptitude in being trained up to this point, he should be able to learn most of these behaviors, depending upon his nature and aptitude. These are only a few of the tricks your cat can learn, however, if you have the patience and time, and if Tiger has the desire to learn. Use your imagination to come up with others that will amaze your friends and challenge your cat.

For these tricks, it's often helpful to incorporate a hand signal as well as a verbal command. Since cats rely so heavily on body language to communicate with other cats, a gestural command is often useful when reinforcing the behavior and trying to get Tiger to perform when you are standing some distance from him.

You will need a clicker and treats for this training.

Shaking Hands

Some cats, those that hate having their feet touched, will not take to this trick very well. In fact, most cats dislike having their feet handled, so you must be careful not to shake Tiger's paw too hard or he may not be willing to perform this trick again.

1. Put your cat on the edge of the raised training area and ask him to sit.

2. When he is sitting calmly, say, *"Tiger, shake,"* reach out your hand, and lift his right paw, using *your* right hand. Don't hold your hand closed around his paw; just rest the paw in your palm. Click the clicker immediately, offer him a treat, and say, *"Shake, good shake."* This is a trick where the clicker/spoon method will come in handy (see page 92) because it's hard to lift the paw, click the clicker, and reward the cat at the same moment without it. Immediately after rewarding Tiger,

After lifting Tiger's paw, reward and say "Shake, good shake!"

let his paw go. Practice this step several times a day for two weeks.

3. After two weeks, Tiger should have connected his paw being lifted with the click and the treat. Now you'll ask him to lift his paw by himself. Show the food reward and say, *"Tiger, shake,"* and move your hand close to your cat's paw without

Some cats just don't like this trick, no matter how tempting the treat. If so, try another trick instead.

touching it. If he lifts his paw, even a little bit, take it in your hand and immediately click, reward, and praise. If not, hook one finger around the back of the cat's leg and tap it forward lightly. He should lift his paw then. Take his paw, click, reward, and praise. Practice every day until Tiger confidently offers his paw to the *shake* command.

Waving

This trick is the easiest of all, since cats naturally investigate things with their paws. Pooka has learned this trick so well that whenever she wants a treat, she waves frantically to get my attention.

1. Put your cat on the edge of the raised training area and ask him to sit and then stay.

2. Stand just out of reach, show the cat that you have a treat, and say, *"Tiger, wave."* Tempt him by holding the treat just out of reach at the level of his face and moving it back and forth. This back-and-forth motion will be your hand signal. If he stands up or moves from the sitting position, ask him to sit again, and then repeat the *wave* command and the gesture. Likely, after you tempt Tiger with the treat, he will reach toward the treat with one paw. When he does, click the clicker, give the treat, and say, *"Wave, good wave."* Practice several times a day just before mealtime.

3. When your cat learns the command and the behavior, stand farther away and give the command.

Kissing

This trick is easy to teach your cat as long as you have an assistant— we'll call her Sue—who doesn't mind having baby food smeared on her face. You'll need a sticky treat that you can dab on Sue's cheek; meat baby food is the best for this since it's gooey and not as disgusting as smearing on cat food.

1. Seat Sue at the raised training area so Tiger can easily reach her cheek. Your assistant should be someone your cat knows and trusts. Smear a bit of the baby food on Sue's cheek. If you don't have an assistant willing to help you out, you can teach Tiger to kiss your cheek.

2. Lift your cat and show him the yummy treat on your obliging assistant's cheek. Place him on the training area a foot or so away from her cheek and say, *"Tiger, kiss!"* Hopefully, Tiger will walk over and lick at the food. If so, click and give him another different and very special treat, and say, *"Kiss, good kiss."* If not, have Sue move closer and closer until Tiger responds correctly. Click, reward, and praise. The other treat is very important because you'll be removing the face food as time goes on. Practice several times a day, or as many times as Sue will sit still for it, for at least a week.

3. Decrease the amount of food on Sue's cheek each day, gradually, as long as your cat is performing the behavior and seems to grasp the idea. Be sure to do it slowly enough,

If Tiger stands up to reach the treat when learning the wave command,, start over with the sit command.

at least over several weeks, so that the treat you give immediately after the proper behavior becomes the motivating factor.

4. Eliminate the food on Sue's face. Tiger should now understand what is expected of him and should lick the cheek to gain the reward. If not, go back a step.

Soon Tiger will associate the gesture with the wave command.

Your assistant should be someone your cat knows and trusts.

If no assistant is available, you can teach Tiger to kiss your face.

5. Gradually increase the distance your cat must go to reach your assistant. If you do it slowly enough, and make the reward motivating enough, eventually you'll be able to get him to cross the room on command and give Sue a kiss.

6. Now train Tiger to give someone else a kiss, so he learns that "kiss" doesn't just mean Sue. To do this, you'll have to go back to the food-on-the-face routine at first, but you should be able to wean Tiger very quickly.

Speaking

Some cats will take to this easily, while others will not take to it at all; it depends upon Tiger's temperament and vocal tendencies. If he is just not a vocalizer, you'll have to be very patient to get the idea across. If he talks to you a lot, teaching this trick will be a snap.

1. Put Tiger on the edge of the raised training area and ask him to sit. You should try this right before dinner when he is hungry. Get a very special treat and let him smell it, then hold it over his head and say, *"Tiger, speak!"* Continue tempting him with the treat; you are hoping he will meow. As soon as he makes any sort of sound, click, reward, and say, *"Speak, good speak."* Try it again. This time, Tiger should speak up more quickly. Practice several times to reinforce the idea.

2. Practice twice a day, but vary the time. You don't want him to think this trick is only a mealtime behavior. Vary the place in which you practice, too. Within a couple of weeks, Tiger should speak on command.

Begging

This trick needs no introduction and is often a big hit. The goal is to get Tiger to sit up on his haunches as though begging for a treat, but not rise up all the way on his hind feet. It's best to use the command *"Beg"* rather than *"Sit up"* so Tiger won't confuse it with the *sit* command.

1. Place your cat on the raised training area and give him the *sit* command. Let him see and smell the treat in your hand, then say, *"Tiger, beg!"* while moving the treat a few inches directly above his head. Don't hold it too high or he will rise up on his hind feet to get to it, and don't hold it too low or he may grab for it. When he rears back on his haunches, which he will likely do, immediately click the clicker, give the reward, and say, *"Beg, good beg."* If he rises to his feet, or reaches for the food with his paws, don't click or reward. Start over. Ideally, you want the cat sitting back on his haunches and holding his paws in front of him in the begging position. Practice several times a day before meals for at least two weeks.

2. When your cat understands the command and the expected behavior, back away a bit and give the command to make sure he really gets it. Continue making the gesture

Tempt Tiger with a treat—he'll get the idea quickly if he's naturally vocal.

For this trick, you want Tiger to sit on his haunches rather than stand up on his hind feet.

with your hand; this becomes your hand signal for this trick. At this point, vary the location of the trick. Now you can ask Tiger to beg wherever he happens to be.

Jumping Through a Hoop

This one isn't as hard as it might seem, since cats are good jumpers and are agile and graceful. You will need special equipment, however: two very sturdy stools or chairs and a hoop that you can hold in your hand and also mount on a support stand so it stays upright. Hoops and stands can be purchased at some

For this trick, overturned wastepaper baskets, painted and weighed at the bottom for safety, can be used as professional-looking props.

pet supply stores—look in the dog section—but you can also make your own. The necessary materials can usually be found by making several trips to your local toy or hardware store. An old piece of garden hose cut and shaped into a circle will do, as will a hula hoop or the plastic tubing available at any hardware store. Just make sure the hoop is big enough for Tiger to jump through without bringing the hoop down on himself. If you can't find or make a stand that will hold the hoop securely, you can improvise by taping the hoop between two chairs. Set up the hoop so that the two stools are on either side of the hoop and about 6 inches (15 cm) away. The hoop should be slightly higher than the stools.

1. Lay the hoop next to Tiger's feeding dishes so he can get used to the sight and smell of it. Do this for a week. After the first two days, lean the hoop up against the wall so Tiger can get used to the hoop in that position. Be sure it can't fall on him; you may want to secure it with tape.

2. Set up your equipment and place the cat on one of the stools. Stand behind the other stool holding a treat, on the other side of the hoop. Reach through the hoop, let your cat smell the treat, and say, *"Tiger, jump!"* Then draw your hand through the hoop and coax him to follow. If he does, immediately click, reward, and say, *"Jump, good jump."* If he tries to go around the hoop by jumping down from the stool, don't click or reward. Place him on the stool and try again. Practice several times a day until Tiger readily steps through the hoop.

3. Gradually lengthen the distance between the two stools so that your cat can no longer just step through the hoop, but must jump. Do this gradually so Tiger won't be afraid and won't misjudge the jump. If he leaps and falls, you may not be able to get him to try it again, but cats are naturally good jumpers and should take to this step without too much trouble.

4. If you have the equipment to do so, raise the height of the hoop and the stools to make the leap even more impressive. Do so gradually.

5. Now teach your cat to jump through with you or an assistant holding the hoop. Tiger should learn to jump wherever the hoop may be. If he has learned the trick well, you shouldn't have a problem moving from the previous step to this one, but you may have to urge him through by waving the treat. Don't allow him to get away with going under or around the hoop, however. Be sure not to click or reward. If necessary, go back a step.

Fetching

This trick will come very naturally to some cats; others will never learn it. Siamese and other Oriental breeds and Abyssinians tend to be more receptive to this trick, as are those breeds with strong hunting instincts. And some cats will sur-

Many cats enjoy fetching and will readily return the ball for repeated throwing.

prise you; Bitty taught *me* this trick—I had nothing to do with it. The reward for her is the enjoyment of chasing the ball and bringing it back to me to throw again.

You need a toy that your cat is very fond of and that he can easily carry in his mouth. Sponge rubber "golf balls" and soft plush balls are good choices. Toys with catnip should be avoided for this trick; getting Tiger stoned won't improve his concentration. You'll need a handful of small treats. It's also very helpful if your cat knows the *come* command before trying this trick.

1. Choose a time of day when your cat is active, such as morning or early evening, before mealtime. Entice him with the toy. When you have his interest, throw the toy a few feet away while saying, *"Tiger, fetch!"* Your cat will probably follow and pounce on the toy. If he does, click the clicker, give him a treat, and say, *"Fetch, good fetch."* Practice this step several times a day for a week.

2. Encourage Tiger to pick up the ball, perhaps by smearing a bit of food on it. If he picks up the ball, click immediately, and offer a treat. When he drops the ball to take the treat, have your hand positioned so the ball falls into your palm. Practice this several times a day for at least a week, or until Tiger is reliably picking up the ball and dropping it for the treat.

3. Throw the ball a few feet away and give the verbal command. When he picks up the ball, say, *"Tiger, come!"* If he makes any move toward you, or even looks at you, click and treat. Don't force him to come; he must decide to come on his own if this is to work. The goal during this step is to make Tiger come a little closer each day before giving the reward. Remember not to throw the ball more than a few feet away so you can control the action.

You may find that your cat drops the ball when he comes to you. If this happens, don't click or reward. Go back a step. He must hold the ball to get the reward. Practice several times a day; this step may take several weeks or longer and you need to be patient. Your cat may take a long time to understand what you expect of him.

4. When Tiger is reliably picking up the ball and bringing it to you, increase the distance of your throw a little at a time. Take this step slowly, because the farther away your cat gets, the harder it will be to reward promptly and catch the ball in your hand. Continue to practice until you can throw the ball across the room and have Tiger return it to you.

Chapter Twelve

Cats on Stage

The cat is, above all things, a dramatist.

—Margaret Benson

The Broadway theater production *Cats,* a musical celebration of the mystery and charm of our feline friends, now holds the honor of being the longest-running Broadway musical. This production is based on *Old Possum's Book of Practical Cats,* a collection of poems that the author, T. S. Eliot, considered not a serious work but playful verses written for his godchildren. However, Eliot is likely to be as well remembered for this book of poems as for his most serious work, "The Wasteland." The fact that this production has run so long in both Britain and the United States is a credit to the charm of T. S. Eliot's verses, and the appeal of cats themselves. Even folks who are less enthused by our feline friends than we are find themselves moved by the magic of this musical celebration of cats.

Cats themselves, however, made their way to stage and screen many years before they were immortalized on stage in *Cats.* The Romans are credited with the first circuses featuring cats, if "credited" is the correct word for the Romans' treatment of the animals. However, the modern type of trained cat performance didn't really catch on until the 1800s, at which time a number of trainers developed domestic cat acts that they performed at theaters and playhouses. In the 1820s a man named Signor Cappelli from Tuscany toured Europe with a troupe of "learned cats" that on cue performed such feats as grinding coffee, sharpening knives, playing music, ringing bells, and other "wonderful amusements." Around the end of the 1800s George Techow and his "wonderful performing cats" amazed audiences with such tricks as leaping obstacles, walking tightropes, and carrying mice, rats, and birds on their backs without attempting to harm them. However, many cat shows merely exhibited rare and beautiful cats, since training cats to perform was as time-consuming and difficult then as it is today.

Circus acts also became popular in the early 1800s. These acts featured big cats—lions, tigers, and leopards, usually—and emphasized the wildness and dangerousness of the big felines as well as the cats' obedience to the trainers. American trainer T. A. van Amburgh is credited with introducing the first wild cat act to accompany his more mundane horse and acrobat show.

Today's Performing Cats

While circus acts featuring wild cats still exist, live public performances of performing domestic cats are rare today. Exceptions include such acts as the Friskies Cat Team sponsored by the Friskies Petcare Company. Usually performing at cat shows and other animal-related exhibitions, the team wows crowds with tricks such as playing the piano, dunking miniature balls into basketball hoops, walking tightropes, running through tunnels, and jumping through hoops. The cats in the team are managed by a professional animal training agency called Critters of the Cinema, and are "spokescats" for Friskies, appearing in commercials as well as in live performances. All of the cats in the team were rescued from shelters in the Los Angeles area.

Most performing cats today are seen on film. For one thing, cats are mercurial performers, and the film medium is more conducive to cat performers since several takes can be shot to get just the right actions and expressions. For another, television and movies have become much more popular forms of entertainment than live performances. Since 1990 the television and movie production industries have been growing at a rate of 20 percent each year, according to the American Humane Association. The demand for trained animals in commercials, television shows, and movies has grown with the industries.

The popularity of companion animals fuels the demand for animal performers as well; advertisers have found that adorable, photogenic cats have a positive impact on the purchasing public and they are used to sell a multitude of products, services, and causes.

The Fancy Feast cat. Friskies® 1999.

Even considering some negative aspects of the film and television business, the depictions of cats in movies and television have benefitted cats in many ways. Because of our fast and far-reaching communications, the public has access to more information about cats and other animals, creating an ever more animal-conscious population. Entire stations have devoted their programming to animals, with good success. For example, the Discovery Channel's "Animal Planet" has "all animals all the time" programming and the My Pet Television Network offers continuous shows on animals wild and domestic. These and other programs help increase public awareness about companion animals and have provided education about cats, their behavior, health needs, and problems worldwide.

The Life of a Movie Star

The cats you see in movies and commercials are usually owned or managed by established trainers who work and live in Hollywood or New York, where most movies, television productions, and commercials are produced. Casting directors and advertising agencies call the professional trainers when the script calls for particular animals. After the trainer gets an idea of what kind of behaviors will be required from the cat, the trainer generally will send photos of the most qualified cats so casting directors can choose the look they want.

Such trainers have stables of cats trained with specific commands and behaviors that they are likely to need on the set. *"Come"* is one of the most important commands for a Hollywood cat, because it is the one most often requested by directors. Any time you see a cat moving from one spot to another, you are seeing the cat responding to the *come* command of the trainer somewhere off screen. "Hitting a mark," where the cat goes to a specific spot to perform her tricks, is another important behavior. This is obviously important when you have the cameras focused on a particular place. *"Stay"* is important, too; you don't want to spend valuable time chasing the cat around the set.

Many of the tricks outlined in the previous chapters are standards for the acting cat. Other behaviors can include playing dead, rolling over, crawling, spinning, jumping into a person's lap or arms, climbing ladders, balancing on beams or wires, opening doors, and interacting with other animals. It's important for acting cats to be able to do their tricks reliably even when the trainer is some distance away, since the trainer must cue the action from off camera.

In the professional cat-training world, it's generally recognized that while dogs can learn to do many tricks and perform them well most of the time, cats tend to do a few tricks consistently, depending on their individual talents, personalities, and

Friskies Cat Team member "Spencer" scores on a slam dunk to demonstrate his basketball playing abilities. Friskies® 1999.

abilities. When you see a cat performing on TV or in the movies, many times you are actually seeing several cats that look alike. Professional animal-training agencies such as Critters of the Cinema, a California-based company that supplies Hollywood with some of their trained animals, usually employ teams of cats similar in appearance. If they need a cat, for instance, that can run across the top of a fence, fetch, and roll over, three different cats may perform these tricks.

Also, cats are less predictable than dogs. A command that the cat obeyed beautifully today may get a blank stare tomorrow. Since time is money in the film industry, well-trained animal actors that perform reliably are always in demand. However, most cat actors are professionals that perform on cue every time. Almost.

For example, in the feature movie *Star Trek: Generations,* the script called for several scenes with Spot, the cat companion of the android crew member Commander Data. Spot was actually played by Brandy and Monster, two orange tabbies that look alike. The requirements of the scene dictated which cat was used. For example, early in the film, the more active Monster jumps off a table and rubs up against Commander Data. Later, when a dirty and scared Spot is rescued from the wreckage of the Enterprise, the more placid Brandy plays the role. During the run of the television show *Star Trek: The Next Generation,* Spot was also a regular and appeared in a number of episodes. Five different orange tabby cats played the character, depending on the demands of the script.

In the early seasons of Star Trek: The Next Generation, Spot was played by a ruddy Somali cat. Somewhere along the line he went through an amazing metamorphosis and transformed into a shorthaired orange tabby. Perhaps an unfortunate transporter accident, or perhaps the producers didn't think the cat-loving audience would notice the difference. They noticed.

It takes more than good training to be a good performing cat. Not only do the felines need to respond reliably to the commands, they must also work well in environments filled with distractions and loud noises. It takes a special cat to be calm and collected in the presence of all the sounds from cameras and crew, actors and actresses, directors, and the myriad other people involved in film production. That's another reason teams of cats are used. If one cat balks, another can step in to fill her place.

When a particular look or breed is needed, such as the hairless Sphynx used in the movie *Austin Powers: International Man of Mystery,* the trainer may go on a talent search for cats that fit the bill. Some trainers keep files of animals that are available for hire and that possess useful talents or abilities. So, if Fluffy is well trained, attractive, and calm around strangers and commotion, she just might have a chance at a Hollywood career. Don't count on it, though— the animal actor business is just as competitive as the human acting profession. A connection with a Hollywood professional trainer is the key to getting Fluffy in the limelight. And even if Fluffy performs her tricks perfectly at home, she may become frightened when taken from her familiar, safe environment. Performing cats require training in handling distracting situations, as well as dispositions suited to the acting life. Training cats to handle these conditions is a full-time job. Location is also important. If you live outside the New York or Los Angeles area, there's little call for animal actors. Of course, Fluffy will always be the star of your show, even if she doesn't break into commercials.

It's nice to know that quite a few of the cats we see on the screen today are felines rescued from that final walk down a shelter's death row. In addition to the Friskies "spokescats," Morris the finicky 9-Lives cat and his two successors, Morris II and III, were all adopted from animal shelters. Catzilla, who made his screen debut in the DreamWorks film *Mouse Hunt,* was adopted from the Los Angeles Humane Society. The cat actor in the Disney film *That Darn Cat* also was found in an L.A. shelter. Many of the trainers who provide cats for the cinema make an effort to include cats from shelters and humane societies in their stables of feline actors.

Friskies Cat Team member "Zoe" leaps at the chance to show off her hurdling skills. Friskies® 1999.

Performing-Animal Abuse

In the early days of performing animals, little protection against abuse existed. Often, the treatment of circus animals was cruel and many trainers relied on harsh methods to gain the animals' cooperation. Bears, elephants, and other animals were often beaten, stabbed, and burned in order to coerce them to perform. While big cats usually didn't respond to such treatment with obedience, and therefore such "training" was usually useless, few trainers understood the feline's nature. Living conditions for these performing animals were usually substandard; when not performing, they were often locked in tiny cages without access to proper food and water. In the 1800s animal lovers began to form organizations to protect animals from abuses.

Unfortunately, abuses of performing animals still exist today. Organizations such as the Performing Animals Welfare Society (PAWS) have been formed to expose and end performing-animal abuse. PAWS runs an animal sanctuary for rescued performing animals such as elephants, bobcats, bears, cougars, leopards, and lions.

Organizations such as the People for the Ethical Treatment of Animals (PETA) were formed to increase public awareness of the treatment of animals and to effect changes in the way we use them. These organizations feel that animals are not ours to do with as we please, but living beings with rights of their own. Some animal advocates even believe that domestication of any kind is unacceptable, including the keeping of companion animals, and see no difference between training tigers to jump through hoops and training domestic cats to perform in movies and commercials.

On the other hand, many animal lovers feel that as long as the animals are happy, well cared for, and enjoy the experience, training and performing do not negatively affect them. In fact, these activities can enhance their quality of life by stimulating them, giving them feelings of accomplishment, and allowing them quality time with their human handlers.

As with all issues dealing with animal rights, the ethics of keeping and training animals is not clear-cut and simple—plenty of gray areas exist between the black-and-white thinking of both the staunch protectors of animals and those who would exploit them for profit. Still, the ethical difference between training tigers to perform in circuses and training domestic cats to perform in movies and television productions, or training them to be better companions, seems clear. Domestic cats have had several thousand years of adaptation to life with humans and while they have certainly had tough times at our hands, ultimately, the relationship has been a mutually beneficial one. Cats enjoy their relationships with humans when those associations are positive. Wild animals taken from their natural environments don't have the centuries of domestication that allow them to accept and enjoy close association with humans.

Also, the living conditions of the animals must be considered. Tigers being moved from city to city to perform must be kept in small cages by necessity, and therefore rarely get the freedom to move around as they would in their natural environment. Domestic cats, on the other hand, are already in their natural environment; when not performing, most go home with their owners or trainers.

The American Humane Association

In the early days of cinema, before computers and sophisticated special effects techniques, the animal action in film was even more dangerous to humans and animals alike than it is today, and animals were subjected to neglect, abuse, and dangerous working conditions. Treated as props rather than sentient beings with feelings like our own, animals were injured or even killed to "get the shot." In those days, no organization was authorized to oversee cinematic productions and ensure good treatment of the animal actors that couldn't speak for themselves.

That changed in 1939, when a horse was deliberately killed during the filming of the Western movie *Jesse James*. A stunt man rode the horse off a 70-foot (21-m) -high cliff into a treacherous white water river to get the needed shot. The stunt man survived, but the horse died in the raging river. Public outcry over this and other animal mistreatment by the industry caused the American Humane Association (AHA) to open an office in the Hollywood area to establish protection for animals in movies. Founded in 1877, the AHA was originally formed to protect both abused children and animals. In addition to the television and film unit, it has divisions for child protection, animal protection, and a Washington, D.C. office. The television and film unit's goal is to ensure the humane treatment of the animals used in movies, television productions, and commercials.

In 1940 the Hayes Office, which restricted objectionable action in movies, recommended that an AHA representative be consulted on every production in which animal actors were used. The AHA reached an agreement with the Motion Picture Association of America (MPAA), which gave the organization authority to serve as a watchdog group on the behalf of animal actors. The AHA dramatically improved the conditions for animal actors.

Although the organization lost its authority in 1966 when the Hayes Office was abolished, it continued to oversee animal action, and a 1980 contract with the Screen Actor's Guild (SAG) and the Alliance of

Motion Picture and Television Producers (AMPTP) again authorized the AHA to monitor animal action in film and television productions. With the popularity of such animal movies as *Homeward Bound: The Incredible Journey* and *Babe,* and given the number of movies, television shows, and commercials with animal action produced each year (more than 850 in 1997), the AHA's job is an immense one. The AHA is not paid for its services to the movie industry, since that would create a conflict of interest. Rather, it is funded by dues, grants, and donations.

Besides being on hand during the shoot to observe animal treatment, the AHA also reviews scripts for productions involving animals to identify potential problems, and works with the directors, trainers, and producers before filming begins to ensure the safety of the animals. This approach prevents problems before they begin. AHA representatives might suggest a better way to get the shot, or suggest the use of animatronics, fake animals, or other techniques to simulate the animal rather than endanger a living one. The AHA also screens movies before release and assigns each a rating based on the treatment of animals in the production. Only the movies that earn an "acceptable" rating are allowed to display the end-credit disclaimer that lets the viewer know no animal was harmed in the making of the movie. Since today's savvy animal-loving moviegoers watch for the disclaimer, production companies are motivated

to earn the rating. However, most production studios welcome the AHA's input and cooperate with the organization. The next time you see a movie with animal actors, sit through all the credits and see if the movie has the AHA disclaimer. Ratings and film reviews are posted on the group's web site (see Useful Addresses and Literature, page 155) and published in the organization's magazine, *The Advocate.*

A Final Word

The methods and techniques covered in this book are based on sound behavioral principles. Use this book as your guide to developing a close and loving relationship with your feline friend; however, only you know your cat's unique temperament and nature, so adjust your socialization and training efforts accordingly. Every cat and every relationship is different; what works with one cat may not work with another. As with all relationships, it will take time to develop a bond with your cat. You'll make mistakes as you go; all cat owners do. Don't worry about them too much; just resolve to do better in the future. If you've developed a bond of trust and love with Fluffy, she'll forgive you. She will make mistakes as well. That's how we all learn.

If your cat can't learn tricks, or doesn't want to, don't force the issue. It's not her fault; she isn't refusing to obey just to spite you. Cats are individuals and some are simply not good candidates for training. That doesn't mean they aren't fine companions. And keep your expectations reasonable; don't expect Fluffy to learn to catch Frisbees in midair or leap into your swimming pool after a tossed ball. Avoid tricks that go against your cat's basic nature—there are some things cats just won't do. Remember, your cat must *want* to do the trick or it's a no go. Developing a "you're going to learn or else!" attitude will get you nowhere. Nothing will be gained by turning training into a battle of wills; you cat simply will not respond and you will damage the trust she feels for you. Keep it light and fun and both of you will enjoy it, even if you don't end up turning Fluffy into a movie star. The object of training is to communicate with your cat and develop a stronger bond of affection and trust, which is, after all, what it's all about.

Respect your cat's unique nature and you'll have a loving companion for life.

Glossary

Adaptation: a change in form, structure, or function that increases an animal's chances of survival within a particular environment.

Ailurophile: a cat lover.

Ailurophobe: a person who hates or fears cats.

Allogrooming: mutual grooming performed between felines.

Alter: to spay or neuter a cat.

Anthropomorphizing: ascribing human characteristics to animals or inanimate objects.

Arrector muscles: small muscles attached to whiskers and hairs that allow them to be moved. The arrector muscles allow the cat's hair to stand up when the cat is alarmed.

Atrichial sweat glands: glands that produce watery sweat to aid in keeping the body cool.

Auditory: relating to hearing or sound.

Awn: a secondary hair type coarser than the down hairs; these hairs form an insulating layer.

Behavior: the actions or reactions of animals in response to internal or external stimuli.

Behavioral shaping: training techniques used to teach complex behaviors that use reinforcement and extinction to modify the initial behavior into another form.

Behaviorism: a form of psychology that views mental illness as maladaptive learned behaviors that can be unlearned.

Benching: the area of the show hall where exhibitors display their cats.

Benching cage: the cage in which exhibitors display their cats while waiting for judging.

Binocular vision: a visual setup in which the eyes face forward and are located forward on the head. The field of vision of each eye partially overlaps the other, allowing good depth perception.

Bloodline: a group of cats related by ancestry or pedigree.

Breed: a group of related cats that share similar physical characteristics and ancestry.

Calico: a cat with patches of black, red, and white.

Calling: a sound made by a female cat in heat; it signals her sexual readiness.

Carnivore: meat eater.

Carpal pad: a pad of tough, hairless skin partway up the cat's foot.

Carrier: A cat carrying an unexpressed recessive gene that is able to pass that gene on to its offspring; also can mean a container used to transport cats.

Cat fancy: the group of people, associations, clubs, and registries involved in the showing and breeding of cats.

Cat show: an event, usually held on the weekend, where cats are shown and judged.

Chemical senses: the senses of smell and taste.

Circadian rhythms: the biological rhythms that determine the pattern of sleep and wakefulness.

Classical conditioning: a method of modifying behavior by associating a secondary stimulus repeatedly with a primary stimulus. A cat associating the sound of a clicker with getting a treat is an example of classical conditioning.

Clicker: a small usually metal and plastic device that makes a clicking sound, used in animal training.

Clubbing: a little-understood feline behavior in which cats gather at a meeting area to socialize.

Compulsive disorders: disorders that cause excessively repeated behavior patterns that have no apparent purpose; also called stereotypic behavior or obsessive-compulsive disorders.

Conditioned response: a reflex in which the response is produced by a secondary stimulus repeatedly being associated with a primary stimulus.

Conformation: the physical type of the cat, which includes coat length, color, bone structure, facial type, and many other factors.

Continuous reinforcement: a schedule of reinforcement in which the animal is rewarded every time it performs a behavior correctly.

Contralateral: a gait in which the right front leg moves forward with the left hind leg, and the left front leg moves forward with the right hind leg.

Core territory: the territory that a cat claims as its sole property and will defend from all intruders.

Correction: negative reinforcement designed to discourage unwanted behavior.

Crepuscular: most active at dawn and dusk.

Declawed: describing a cat that has had its claws surgically removed. Some associations don't allow declawed cats to be shown.

Digitigrade: walking on the toes and ball of the foot only. Cats are digitigrade.

Displacement behavior: an activity such as grooming that helps the animal cope with conflict or relieve feelings of fear, embarrassment, or anger.

Distress purring: purring that occurs when the cat is experiencing discomfort. Researchers believe cats can purr in response to any strong emotion.

Domestic cat: a nonpedigreed cat.

Domestication: a process in which a species becomes docile and dependent upon humankind.

Dominance hierarchy: the social structure of cats, in which cats use confrontations to determine their places in the society. The dominant cat claims the most territory.

Dominant: a genetic trait that masks the effects of recessive genes; also the top cat in the cat hierarchy.

Down: a secondary hair type that is soft and slightly wavy; much shorter than guard hairs.

EEG: electroencephalograph, a device that measures the rhythmic electrical activity of the brain.

Epoch: a subdivision of a geologic period.

Estrus: see **heat.**

Evolution: the development of a species or organism from a primitive state to a more specialized, complex state.

Extinction: behaviors that become less frequent and finally cease for lack of reinforcement; also means when a species ceases to exist.

Fel d1: an allergenic protein secreted by saliva and sebaceous glands. It causes allergic reactions in some people.

Felidae: the cat family.

Feline AIDS: a disease that attacks the domestic cat's immune system. While similar to human AIDS, it cannot be spread to humans or other animal species. See **feline immunodeficiency virus (FIV).**

Feline infectious peritonitis: see **FIP.**

Feline leukemia virus (FeLV): a highly infectious virus that causes feline leukemia, one of the most deadly and widespread domestic feline diseases. FeLV weakens the immune system so that in the secondary stage of the disease, the cat dies of FeLV-related diseases such as cancer.

Feline immunodeficiency virus (FIV): the virus that causes feline AIDS; it attacks the domestic cat's immune system. While similar to human HIV, it cannot be spread to humans or other animal species. See **feline AIDS.**

Felis silvestris libyca: a species of cat called the African wildcat that's the closest ancestor of the domestic cat; it lives in Africa, Western Asia, Scotland, and Southern Europe.

Felis catus: the species of domestic cat.

FeLV: see **feline leukemia virus.**

Feral: a domesticated animal that has reverted to the wild or that has been born in the wild.

FIP: feline infectious peritonitis; a highly contagious disease caused by a coronavirus; it's almost always fatal to domestic cats.

Flehmen response: the facial expression seen when a cat's Jacobson's organ is stimulated.

Genes: units of heredity that control growth, development, and function of organisms.

Genetics: the study of genes and heredity.

Genotype: the genetic composition of a cat, whether or not expressed in the physical appearance.

Guard hairs: the longest of the three hair types; they form the coat's outer layer.

Habitat: the natural environment of a particular plant or animal.

Heat: the sexual cycle of the female cat.

High-rise syndrome: the term given for injuries sustained when an animal falls from a substantial height.

Home range: the area in which the cat hunts and explores, which usually overlaps the ranges of other cats. The size depends on the allotment of shelter and food.

Household Pet (HHP): a random-bred cat, or a purebred cat that is not registered or cannot compete with members of its breed. These cats compete in a special category called the Household Pet or HHP category.

Hyperesthesia: a rare feline disorder in which the cat has sudden bouts of frantic racing, yowling, twitching, licking, and other aberrant behavior.

Inbreeding: mating two closely related cats, such as parent to child or brother to sister.

Induced ovulator: an animal that must have sexual contact for ovulation to occur.

Innate behavior: inborn instinctual behavior that's genetically programmed into animals.

Instinct: a powerful, inborn impulse or pattern of behavior characteristic to a species, often in response to specific environmental stimuli.

Interestrus: the period of ovarian and sexual inactivity following estrus.

Intermittent reinforcement: a schedule of reinforcement in which the animal is rewarded intermittently when it performs a behavior correctly.

Irritable aggression: aggression that occurs when the cat becomes annoyed; can be caused by overstimulation during play, grooming, petting, or other activities.

Jacobson's organ: a sensory organ in the roof of the cat's mouth that collects information from tastes and smells.

Kneading: a behavior in which a kitten kneads its mother's belly to facilitate milk production; this behavior is also often seen in adult cats that march up and down with their front feet while digging in their claws, usually on their owners' laps.

Learned behavior: behavior that is learned from contact with the environment rather than being inborn.

Litter: a family of kittens; can also mean matter used as cat toilet material.

Lordosis: the mating position of the female cat, in which the cat crouches with back swayed and tail held to one side.

Motivational imperative: the driving force that motivates all behavior; for example, the need to survive.

Multicat household: a household that contains more than one cat.

Mutation: a change in a gene that results in a change in hereditary characteristics between two generations.

Natural selection: a process in which the weaker members of a species do not survive, while the stronger members thrive and produce offspring.

Negative reinforcement: a method of shaping behavior that administers negative results for undesirable behavior. For example, if the subject performs an undesired behavior, a punishment or correction is given to make it less likely that the behavior will be repeated.

Neurotransmitters: the chemicals responsible for transmitting nerve impulses.

Neutering: while often applied only to male cats, the term can mean either castrating male cats or removing the female cat's ovaries, fallopian tubes, and uterus (spaying).

Nocturnal: describing an animal that is primarily active at night.

Obsessive-compulsive disorders: see **compulsive disorders.**

Olfactory: relating to the sense of smell.

Olfactory mucosa: the area of the nasal passages responsible for the detection of scents.

Operant conditioning: a method of modifying behavior using reinforcement of desirable behaviors and punishment of undesirable behaviors. An example of this kind of conditioning would be rewarding a cat with a treat for sitting on command.

Overspecialization: when an animal adapts to a certain environment to such an extent that it can no longer adjust to environmental changes.

Pack behavior: a hierarchical social order in which the animals cooperate in a coordinated manner to increase the likelihood of survival.

Papers: usually, a cat's pedigree or certificate of registration.

Papillae: small bumps that cover the feline tongue. Some carry taste buds, while others serve other functions, such as rasping meat off bones.

Passive negative reinforcement: negative reinforcement that the cat doesn't associate with the trainer. An example of passive negative reinforcement is putting Bitter Apple or Tabasco sauce on the leaves of houseplants. The bitter taste discourages the behavior and the cat doesn't connect the trainer with the unpleasant consequences.

Pattern: the color distribution on a cat's coat that forms a particular pattern, such as the striped tabby pattern.

Pheromone: chemical substance released by an animal that influences the sexual behavior of other animals of the same species. Pheromones are chemical messages that attract potential mates.

Photocycle: the changing cyclical periods of sunlight and darkness.

Plantigrade: walking on the entire foot rather than on the toes and ball. Humans are plantigrade.

Polydactyl: having extra toes on one or more feet.

Polygenes: groups of genes, small in effect individually, that act together to produce greater bodily characteristics.

Positive reinforcement: a method of shaping behavior that administers positive results for desirable behavior. For example, if the subject performs the desired behavior, a reward is given to make it more likely that the behavior will be repeated.

Predator: an animal that survives by eating the flesh of other animals.

Proestrus: the period before estrus.

Psi-trailing: the cat's as-yet unsubstantiated ability to find its way home to its owners, whose new home is a place the cat has never been.

Purebred cat: a cat whose heritage is documented and registered.

Queen: a breeding female cat.

Rainbow Bridge: the legendary bridge that connects heaven and earth where beloved pets go after death to wait for their human companions to join them.

Random-bred: describing a cat that is not bred intentionally and whose ancestry is not known.

Receptor: a nerve ending that responds to a chemical stimulus; the taste buds, for example, are receptors.

Recessive: describing a characteristic that is unable to express itself in the cat's physical appearance in the presence of the alternate dominant characteristic.

Redirected aggression: aggression directed at an object, animal, or person that is not the cause of the aggressive reaction.

REM: rapid eye movement; refers to the sleep period called active sleep.

Remote negative reinforcement: see **passive negative reinforcement.**

Ritual posturing: one of the ways cats challenge one another. Ritual movements and body positions communicate their intentions and feelings.

Saber-toothed cats: extinct now, the saber-toothed cats were primarily distinguished by the very large daggerlike upper canine teeth.

Scent marking: a means of communication by which a cat leaves urine, feces, and glandular secretions as chemical messages for other cats.

Self-righting reflex: the reflex that allows the cat to right itself in midair.

Sensitive period: the period of a cat's life during which behaviors begin to manifest themselves and during which they are impressionable and susceptible to experiences that will shape their behavior later in life.

Shaping behavior: see **behavioral shaping.**

Sire: father of a kitten or litter.

Smilodon fatalis: a saber-toothed cat found in California that existed about 10,000 years ago.

Spaying: neutering of a female cat.

Spraying: a marking behavior in which the cat sprays urine onto a vertical surface.

Standards: the guidelines that establish the ideal conformation for each breed.

Stimuli: the plural of stimulus; agents, actions, or conditions that elicit a physiological or psychological response or activity.

Survival instinct: the instinct that drives all organisms to protect their own lives or the lives of their offspring or group members.

SWS: slow-wave sleep; refers to the sleep period called quiet sleep.

Tabby: any cat displaying the striped tabby pattern.

Tapetum lucidum: a reflective layer of cells that line the back of the retina, giving nocturnal animals the ability to see well in near darkness.

Territorial boundary: the border of a cat's territory.

Tom: an unneutered male cat.

Tortoiseshell: a cat with patches of black and orange.

Undercoat: the awn and down hairs.

Variable reinforcement: see **intermittent reinforcement.**

Vibrissae: a cat's whiskers. These hairs extend three times deeper into the skin than ordinary hairs, and are very sensitive to touch.

Vomeronasal organ: see **Jacobson's organ.**

Wool sucking: a compulsive disorder that causes the cat to suck, chew, lick, or eat wool or other fabrics.

Useful Addresses and Literature

Associations

American Association of Cat Enthusiasts
(AACE)
P.O. Box 213
Pine Brook, NJ 07058
(973) 335-6717
www.aaceinc.org

American Cat Association (ACA)
8101 Katherine Avenue
Panorama City, CA 91402
(818) 781-5656

American Cat Fanciers Association
(ACFA)
P.O. Box 203
Point Lookout, MO 65726
(417) 334-5430
www.acfacat.com

Canadian Cat Association (CCA)
220 Advance Boulevard, Suite 101
Brampton, Ontario
Canada L6T 4J5
(905) 459-1481
www.cca-afc.com

Cat Fanciers Association (CFA)
P.O. Box 1005
Manasquan, NJ 08736
(732) 528-9797
www.cfainc.org

Cat Fanciers Federation (CFF)
Box 661
Gratis, OH 45330
(937) 787-9009
www.cffinc.org

National Cat Fanciers Association
(NCFA)
10215 West Mount Morris Road
Flushing, MI 48433
(810) 659-9517

The International Cat Association (TICA)
P.O. Box 2684
Harlingen, TX 78551
(956) 428-8046
www.tica.org

Traditional Cat Association, Inc. (TCA)
18509 N.E. 279th Street
Battle Ground, WA 98604

United Feline Organization (UFO)
P.O. Box 3234
Olympia, WA 98509-3234
(360) 438-6903

Organizations and Agencies

American Humane Association (AHA)
63 Inverness Drive East
Englewood, CO 80112-5117
(303) 792-9900
www.AHAfilm.org

AHA Western Regional Office
Film and Television Unit
153 Dickens Street
Sherman Oaks, CA 91403
(818) 501-0123
(800) 677-3420 hotline for animals
    abused on film or movie sets
AHAwest@aol.com

American Society for the Prevention of
    Cruelty to Animals (ASPCA)
424 East 92nd Street
New York, NY 10128
(212) 876-7700

Animal People (nonprofit organization)
The newsletter provides information on
    animal charities and other animal-
    related issues.
P.O. Box 960
Clinton, WA 98236-0960
(360) 579-2505
www.animalpepl.org

Best Friends Animal Sanctuary
Kanab, UT 84741
(801) 644-2001

Cornell Feline Health Center
New York State College of Veterinary
    Medicine
Cornell University
Ithaca, NY 14853

The Delta Society
P.O. Box 1080
Renton, WA 98057
(206) 226-7357

Friends of Animals
P.O. Box 1244
Norwalk, CT 06856
(800) 631-2212 (for low-cost spay/neuter
    program information)

Fund for Animals
200 W. 57th Street
New York, NY 10019
(212) 246-2096

The Humane Society of the United
    States (HSUS)
2100 L Street, N.W.
Washington, DC 20037
(202) 452-1100

People for the Ethical Treatment of
    Animals (PETA)
501 Front Street
Norfolk, VA 23510
(757) 622-PETA
www.peta-online.org

Performing Animal Welfare Society
    (PAWS)
11435 Simmerhorn Road
Galt, CA 95632
(916) 393-7297

Pets Are Wonderful Support (PAWS),
    provides pet-related services for
    people with AIDS
P.O. Box 460489
San Francisco, CA 94146
(415) 241-1460

Robert H. Winn Foundation for
    Cat Health
Established by the CFA
1805 Atlantic Avenue
P.O. Box 1005
Manasquan, NJ 08736-1005
(732) 528-9797

Pet Products and Mail-Order Companies

Clicker training Website
www.clickertraining.com

Doctors Foster & Smith
2253 Air Park Road
P.O. Box 100
Rhinelander, WI 54501-0100
(800) 826-7206

Fe-Lines (Sticky Paws source)
2924 6th Avenue
Fort Worth, TX 76102
(888) 697-2873

New England Serum Company
(Source of SoftPaws)
P.O. Box 128
Topsfield, MA 01983-0228
(800) 637-3786

Pryor, Karen
Clicker Training Start-Up Kit
Sunshine Books
(800) 47CLICK

R.C. Steele Wholesale Pet Supplies
1989 Transit Way, Box 910
Brockport, NY 14420-0910
(800) 872-3773

SoftPaws Website
Dr. Christianne Schelling
www.softpaws.com
(800) 989-2542

Magazines

Cat Fancier's Almanac
P.O. Box 1005
Manasquan, NJ 08736-0805
(908) 528-9797

Cat Fancy
P.O. Box 6050
Mission Viejo, CA 92690
(800) 365-4421
www.catfancy.com

Catnip
Belvoir Publications, Inc.
P.O. Box 420235
Palm Coast, FL 32142
(800) 829-0926

CATS
Primedia, Inc.
Two Park Avenue, 11th Floor
New York, NY 10016
(800) 829-9125
www.catsmag.com

CATsumer Report
P.O. Box 10069
Austin, TX 78766-1069
(800) 968-1738

Cat Watch
Cornell University College of Veterinary
    Medicine
Box 420235
Palm Coast, FL 32142-0235
(800) 829-8893
www.vet.cornell.edu

I Love Cats
450 7th Avenue, Suite 1701
New York, NY 10123

The Whole Cat Journal
P.O. Box 420235
Palm Coast, FL 32142
(800) 829-9165

Books

Behrend, K., and M. Wegler. The Complete Book of Cat Care. Hauppauge, New York: Barron's Educational Series, Inc., 1991.

Behrend, Katrin. *Indoor Cats.* Hauppauge, New York: Barron's Educational Series, Inc., 1999.

Collier, Marjorie McCann. *Siamese Cats, A Complete Pet Owner's Manual.* Hauppauge, New York: Barron's Educational Series, Inc., 1992.

Daly, Carol Himsel, D.V.M. *Caring for Your Sick Cat.* Hauppauge, New York: Barron's Educational Series, Inc., 1994.

Davis, Karen. *Somali Cats, A Complete Pet Owner's Manual.* Hauppauge, New York: Barron's Educational Series, Inc., 1996.

____. *Exotic Shorthair Cats, A Complete Pet Owner's Manual.* Hauppauge, New York: Barron's Educational Series, Inc., 1997.

Frye, Fredric. *First Aid for Your Cat.* Hauppauge, New York: Barron's Educational Series, Inc., 1987.

Gordon, Anne. *Show Biz Tricks for Cats.* Holbrook, Massachusetts: Adams Media Corporation, 1996.

Helgren, J. Anne. *Abyssinian Cats, A Complete Pet Owner's Manual.* Hauppauge, New York: Barron's Educational Series, Inc., 1995.

____. *Encyclopedia of Cat Breeds.* Hauppauge, New York: Barron's Educational Series, Inc., 1997.

____. *Himalayan Cats, A Complete Pet Owner's Manual.* Hauppauge, New York: Barron's Educational Series, Inc., 1996.

Helgren, J. Anne, and Phil Maggitti. *It's Showtime.* Hauppauge, New York: Barron's Educational Series, Inc., 1998.

Muller, Ulrike. *Persian Cats, A Complete Pet Owner's Manual.* Hauppauge, New York: Barron's Educational Series, Inc., 1990.

Pedersen, Niels C. *Feline Husbandry.* Goleta, California: American Veterinary Publications, Inc., 1991.

Robinson, Roy. *Genetics for Cat Breeders.* Oxford, England: Pergamon Press, 1977.

Viner, Bradley, D.V.M. *The Cat Care Manual.* Hauppauge, New York: Barron's Educational Series, Inc., 1986.

Wright, Michael, and Sally Walters, eds. *The Book of the Cat.* New York: Summit Books, 1980.

Index